ARCHAEOLOGICAL SURVEY OF INDIA
NEW IMPERIAL SERIES, VOLUME XXXIV.

PALLAVA ARCHITECTURE

ARCHAEOLOGICAL SURVEY OF INDIA
NEW IMPERIAL SERIES, VOLUME XXXIV.

PALLAVA ARCHITECTURE

BY

ALEXANDER REA, F.S.A. SCOT., M.R.A.S.,

SUPERINTENDENT, ARCHAEOLOGICAL SURVEY DEPARTENT,
SOUTHERN CIRCLE, INDIA, AND
HONORARY ASSISTANT SUPERINTENDENT, GOVERNMENT MUSEUM,
MADRAS.

GYAN

Published by

Gyan Publishing House
5, Ansari Road
Daryaganj, New Delhi-110002
Phone: 011-47034999, 9811692060
E-mail: books@gyanbooks.com

Distribution Network
gyanbooks.com
India, USA, Canada, UK, Australia, France

ISBN : 978-81-212-4621-7 (PB)
First Published, 1909

2nd Impression 2020

Printed at: Gyan Press, Delhi.

ARCHÆOLOGICAL SURVEY OF INDIA.

NEW IMPERIAL SERIES, VOLUME XXXIV.

PALLAVA ARCHITECTURE.

BY

ALEXANDER REA, F.S.A. SCOT., M.R.A.S.,

SUPERINTENDENT, ARCHÆOLOGICAL SURVEY DEPARTMENT,
SOUTHERN CIRCLE, INDIA,

AND

HONORARY ASSISTANT SUPERINTENDENT, GOVERNMENT MUSEUM MADRAS.

MADRAS:
PRINTED BY THE SUPERINTENDENT, GOVERNMENT PRESS.

1909.

CONTENTS.

LIST OF PLATES.

REPORT

OF

THE ARCHÆOLOGICAL SURVEY OF SOUTHERN INDIA.

PALLAVA ARCHITECTURE OF KÂÑCHÎPURAM.

INTRODUCTORY.

KÂÑCHÎPURAM, the ancient capital of the Pallava kingdom, is situated about 30 miles south-west of Madras.

It has from a very early date been noted for the number and beauty of its temples. At the present day it is chiefly remarkable for its larger Dravidian temples, which, however, compared with the earlier examples, are of comparatively recent date; but before 1883, no one imagined that buildings still exist here, which are contemporary with, or earlier than some of the oldest examples of South Indian Hindu architecture hitherto known.

Among the earliest monuments of the South, the most ancient and best known are those at Mâmallâpuram; and, as the *rathas* there, are unmistakable monolithic reproductions of what must have been earlier structural buildings, it became a question whether any examples of these earlier buildings might still exist. Considering the early date of the *rathas*, it was hardly to be expected that any buildings could have withstood the ravages of time and violence from an earlier period. Until within a few years ago, few or no Hindu structural temples in the Peninsula, were known of a date anterior to those of the Chôḷas of the eleventh century.[1] The discovery that the Pallavas were the excavators of the Mâmallâpuram remains, however showed that if any of these earlier structures might still be found, they would likely occur in the country formerly under the sway of the Pallavas, and possibly in their ancient capital itself. But the first to be discovered were the group at Paṭṭadakal in the Belgaum district, of which the temple of Virupaksha dates from the early part of the eighth century A.D. These are described in the first *Report of the Archæological Survey of Western India.* The further discovery of the Kâñchîpuram group of temples now under review is of considerable importance to archæological research, and, with the Paṭṭadakal and Kokanûr temples, supplies a further link which earlier investigators had, previous to 1874, looked for in vain. In 1883, Mr. R. Sewell, I.C.S. (retired), visited Kâñchîpuram, and observed two temples—the Mataṅgêśvara, and Muktêśvara—whose porticos bore a striking resemblance to the façades of some of the cave temples at Mâmallâpuram.[2] The tower also, of another temple—the Vaikuṇṭha Perumâḷ—he noted as having an outline in close affinity to that of the Dharmarâja *ratha* at Mâmallâpuram, each storey being distinctly stepped back from that immediately below it, forming a platform with parapet on each, after the style of the ancient *vihâras*, but common also to many

---

[1] Fergusson: *His. of Ind and East Arch.* p. 336.

[2] *Jour., R.A.S.,* Vol. XVI, Part I.

of the early Dravidian temples. [3] On surveying this building, I noted that the peculiarity referred to, is more complete than even the view from the outside would lead one to expect. The platforms extend right through the tower, forming a series of shrines—one above another,—in which images are placed.

Dr. Burgess afterwards visited the place in 1883 and discovered the Kailâsanâdha temple, a building of much more importance architecturally, than any of those previously noted.

On a subsequent visit, I noted other two Pallava shrines—the Tripurântakêśvara and Airâvatêśvara. These are at present the only known examples of Pallava architecture remaining in the city.

HISTORY AND ARCHITECTURE.

The history of the people to whom we ascribe these monuments is to a great degree very fragmentary, but so far as it bears on the architecture and shows the early extent and power of the Pallava kingdom, it will be desirable to incorporate it in the following sketch.

The state of civilization of a people is judged by its architecture, and in cases such as this, where the other historical records are comparatively scanty, or where they do exist,—sometimes of a doubtful nature, we may find the architecture a useful auxiliary in elucidating many obscure matters of history. Where we find a high state of excellence in the architectural arts at any age and in any country, we may assume as a *sine qua non*, that the people likewise had advanced considerably in civilization.

The capital city of the Pallavas occupies a very prominent place in the ancient history of Southern India, and has been regarded from early times as one of the seven sacred places of India.[4] Until quite lately, the history of that people was, from the absence of reliable data—on which to base any trustworthy conclusions regarding the extent and power of the dynasty—enveloped in uncertainty. The wilful misrepresentation of facts in the legend of the conquest of this kingdom by Adoṇḍai Chôḷa—in order to magnify the successes of that prince—a statement that the conqueror found the country a wilderness inhabited by tribes no better than nomades; and that he founded the city of Kâñchîpuram—is an example of one of the many exploded myths of Indian history. The very legend betrays itself, and shows that underneath the description lies a substratum of fact, which crops out here and there, and which shows that the despised Kurumbars[5] had reached a high pitch of civilization, were good agriculturists and understood the art of war.

---

[3] See Fergusson: *Ind. and East Arch.*, p. 134.   [4] Foulkes: *Salem Manual*, I, p. 10.

[5] The derivation of the word "Kurumbar" is evidently from the same root as the Tamil word குறும்பு (surly). It was used as a term of reproach, meaning that those people were boors, as குறும்பர, (a surly fellow).

The Villâlars also, would seem to have been hunters, and their name derived from வில்லாளன் (a bowman).

The word "Pallava" has been regarded as taken from a Sanskrit word meaning a sprout. I think, however, it is unlikely the name would be of Sanskrit origin as other of their contemporaries were known by Tamil appellations, and their language also was Tamil.

The references made in inscriptions to making the Pallavas "hold the sprout," are only I think, pedantic Pandits' puns, or a play on the double meaning of the word. I would suggest that it might be derived,—by somewhat free translation—from the two Tamil words பால் (milk) and இழு (to pull); referring to their being agriculturists, or milkdrawers—like the Gopalas of the Northern Dekhan. The modern word for "milking" is different, but it may not always have been so. Another, and more probable derivation might be suggested; the masculine singular termination in Tamil is *avan*, and the plural *avar*; now prefixing the word pal (milk) would give *Palavan*; or Palavar as the honorific or plural. *Palavan* in that case, would mean milkman. An inscription at Pallavaram gives the word "Pal(l)avarpuram" meaning "town of the Pallavas." Avar in this case is evidently the third person masculine plural added to the word Pal (l).

According to tradition, Adoṇḍai found a great number of tanks, and water courses constructed at public expense.[6] They were known to have had strong fortresses throughout their country; and, their coast possessed a considerable commerce.[7] Their land was divided into twenty-four parts; divisions which were afterwards adopted by the Chôḷas themselves when they became masters of the country. They had a certain form of religion;[8] and, as the merchants of Kavêripûmpaṭṭanam sought trading intercourse with them, they built certain trading stations, among which are mentioned Kadalúr (Cuddalore), and Sâla-Kupam (Salavankuppam near Mâmallâpuram): they flourished in consequence. During the battle mentioned in the legend, they were sufficiently strong to offer a considerable resistance to Adoṇḍai's army. After that, Śiva appeared in a dream and promised him victory over the Kurumbars. The following day the Kurumbar troops were routed with great slaughter.

As one of the trophies of the fight was stated to be a brazen or bronze gate of the Puṛal fort, it shows that they were also workers in metal. After some more fighting, the other forts were taken, the country subdued and named Toṇḍamaṇḍalam. An analysis of these and other statements should represent what class of people the former rulers were; but the general tenor of the legend has itself been sufficient to obscure for centuries, or entirely blot out from the pages of history, almost the very name of this once great and powerful race. The foregoing quotations from statements which bear a certain amount of historical truth, should therefore be taken with some reserve, as it is hardly necessary to point out how absurd are the inferences which it was intended the tradition should convey, when we consider that it refers to a period in the middle of the eleventh century; while we find from more reliable evidences, that the Pallavas, having been a powerful nation as early, or earlier than the first century of the Christian era, had, at the later date, possibly reached the zenith of their power and fallen into their decline. This legend of the conquerors would have us believe that the conquered race were a primitive and rude people, who had never reached any degree of civilization, but their architecture tells a different tale which any qualified student may read.

The early people had no history properly so called, and where facts were wanting, they invented them to suit their own opinions of what should be.[9] But notwithstanding such perversions, which have been put forth clothed with the appearance of authentic historical truth, the real facts generally come at last to light, and, in this case have done so with a fulness, sufficient to throw in the shade the vaunted greatness of the Chôḷas themselves.

Sir Walter Elliot, by his collection of inscriptions relating to this people, directed attention to the important place the Pallavas had occupied in the early history of Southern India; a fact which had been almost entirely overlooked by previous historians. Certain it is, that architectural works, which we now know to be theirs, were assigned to the Chôḷas, or some other contemporary dynasty. Inscriptions translated in the *Indian Antiquary* added further facts; the Rev. Mr. Foulkes collected the information thus elicited, by his paper in the *Salem District Manual*, and others in various scientific journals. Other inscriptions since discovered, have proved useful additions to our hitherto scanty knowledge of the subject. Materials are therefore now available, to enable us to assign

---

[6] Ellis: *Papers on Mirasi Right*, 1862 Edition, p. 39. [7] Ellis: *Papers on Mirasi Right*, 1862 Edition, pp. 39, 229 and 242.

[8] Foulkes: *Salem Manual*, I, p. 7. Taylor: *Jour., As. Soc. Beng.* VII, 403. Their buildings and the sculptures thereon, show that this "certain form of religion," was exactly the same as that followed by the Chôḷas themselves.

[9] See also Burnell: *S.I. Pal.*, p. VII, note 1.

with a fair approximation to historical exactness, the real position occupied by the Pallavas in their relation to other and better known dynasties.

From the inscriptions already brought to light, we know they occupied a position of considerable influence at, or earlier than the Christian Era. In the fifth century B.C. Gautama Buddha is said to have converted the people of Kâñchîpuram.[10] In the third century B.C, Aśôka, it is said, built many Buddhist Topes in the neighbourhood;[11] no material evidence has however, as yet been found to support the tradition. This is the earliest and almost only record we have of the introduction of Buddhism into the Pallava Country. The early religion of the Pallavas was apparently Buddhism.

Hiuen Thsang probably only related tradition when he spoke of Buddha having personally converted the people. Of the topes said to have been built by Aśôka, none now remain in the neighbourhood of Kâñchîpuram,—though the existing earliest buildings in the country are erected on distinct Buddhist models.

About 150 years later, we find that numerous Buddhist monks from the Pallava country visited Ceylon.[12] In the first century A.D. the Pallavas were ruling in the Southern Dakhan, they built forts and palaces in the basin of the Pâlâr, and carried on an extensive commerce both with the West and East.[13]

The materials for this period are rather scanty for the record of a continuous history; but they are sufficient to show that at this time, the dynasty occupied a position of considerable power and influence.

As indicating the commerce with the West, Roman coins are still found occasionally at the ancient seaport of Mâmallâpuram. Leaden coins also, of the Ândhra kings have been got at the same and other places in the Pallava Country.[14] Baktrian coins, of a date seemingly anterior to the Christian era, have also been found. The Baktrian kingdom was perhaps overthrown about a century B.C.[15] The intercourse which the coins indicate, must therefore be placed about or before that date.

About the same period, Vishnubhûpa reigned at Kâñchîpuram;[16] and later Śâlivâhana an ancestor of Mukunti Pallava is said to have reigned at the same place.[17]

About this time, a large colony is supposed to have emigrated from the coast of Telingâna and settled in Java.[18] An inscription found there, belonging to about the fifth century A.D.[19] is probably the work of this people. Early in our era, Mallêśvara reigned at Mâmallâpuram—which was originally called after his name[20] —and in his reign, the place was destroyed by an inundation of the sea.[21]

It has been mentioned[22] that the ancient Hindu emigration from India to Java came not from the east, but the west coast. In the light of additional information since brought to light, this view must be somewhat modified, as, according to Burnell, the palæographical evidences of the Javanese inscriptions show more connection with the Pallava

---

[10] Sewell; *Lists* I, p. 176, after Hiuen Thsang.
[11] *Ibid.*
[12] Fergusson: *Tree and Serpent Worship*, p. 195. *Ratnâvali*, II, p. 222. Foulkes: *Salem Manual*, I, p. 4. Turnour: *Mahawanso* I, 171.
[13] Foulkes: *Ind. Antiq.*, VIII, 170. *Salem Manual*, I, 3, II, 352. Taylor: *Jour., As. Soc., Bengl.*, VII (II) 111, 112. Sewell: *Lists* I, 172.
[14] Boswell: *Ind. Antiq.*, I, 151. Wilson: *Asiat. Res.* XVIII, 566, 579, 582.
[15] Fergusson: *Ind. and East. Arch.*, pp. 26, 27. Elliot: *Madr. Jour. of Lit. and Sci.*, XIX, 242, 243.
[16] Burgess: *Archl Repts. Un. Ind*, 1876, ch. III. Fleet: *Ind. Antiq.*, VII, 57.
[17] Wilson: *Catl. Macken. Mss.*, 1, p. CXXIV. Rice: *Mys. Ins.*, p. III.
[18] Taylor: *Madr. Jour. Lit. and Sci.*, XVI, 132.
[19] Burnell: *S.I. Palæ.*, p. 131.
[20] Chambers: *As. Res.* I, 156. Taylor: *Madr. Jour. Lit. and Sci.*, VIII, 65, XIII, 39.
[21] Chambers: *As. Res.* I, 156.
[22] Fergusson: *Ind. and Eas. Arch.*, p. 637.

than with those of any other part of India. "The architecture also of the temples in Java, is south—not north—Indian in style."[23] From any inscriptional evidence we have on the point, Mâmallâpuram seems to have been an important seaport in the days of the Pallavas. Fergusson mentions that there is no trace of any city near the excavations that could have been inhabited.[24] This perhaps admits of explanation. During the many centuries that these works have been in existence, the sea has gradually encroached and the sand drifted, till the eastern portion of the courtyard of the "shore" temple has been washed away; (a *dîpdân* is still seen standing in the water). The original floor line of the court is about 12 feet under the present surface of the sand. The caves at Sâluvankuppam are at a considerable depth below the present sand surface; as also the basement of the large *bas relief*, known as "Arjuna's penance;" and other works which stand on a low level. May not then, the ruins of any city there may have been, be under the sand?

Ptolemy's emporium for the Golden chersonese, and the farther east—in the second century—was within the Pallava territory on the eastern coast,[25] and Ârkât, and Mâmallâpuram have respectively been identified with Ptolemy's *Arkati Regio Soræ* and *Malerpha.*[26]

This would show that a very considerable commerce was then being carried on between the East and the West, and, that it must have been in existence even before the time these records refer to. The western coins also, which are found all over the region, show how general this intercourse must have been.

With regard to ancient works of this dynasty in the Ârkât District, I have, in another report, pointed out, that some and probably all of the numerous caves found there, are the works of the Pallavas, showing that the rock excavations executed by them are more numerous and extensive than has been hitherto supposed.[27]

That a high proficiency in the arts did prevail among these people, and at a very early period, is shown by different records. The Pallava kings were renowned for their learning, skill in warfare, and personal valour;[28] and Hiuen Thsang (640 A.D.) found numerous temples throughout the portion of his route which lay through this country; and large and richly sculptured Buddhist buildings at Dhanakata and Pingola. Numerous inscriptions bear similar evidence, and the masses of inscribed documents which have been collected, and are still accumulating, enable us to judge with a fair approximation, of the liberal patronage bestowed by the Pallavas on learning, and the architectural arts, from the earliest times of which we have at present any recorded knowledge of them.

It is but reasonable to suppose that a people who had attained such power and culture, would,—in common with other races of which we have fuller information—have free communication with western nations. That there were trading relations between the East and West has been already shown, (*ib.*); but that this intercourse was so complete, as to make the arts of the one affect those of the other, is what the architecture in several instances would seem to show. We know from the finding of coins, and other sources, that the Romans had trading communication with the Pallavas.

It can be proved that an intimate connection did exist between the north of India and Rome at that time; but with the South, it has hitherto been supposed that only trade was

---

[23] *S.I. Palæ.*, pp. 130 to 134. [24] *Cave temples*, 107–108. [25] Foulkes: *Ind. Antiq.*. VII, 7.

[26] Ellis: *Papers on Mir. Right*, 230, 242. Wilson: *Mack.*, *MSS.* I, p. XXXIV. Caldwell: *Gram. Drav. Lang. Intr.*, p. Gubbins: *Jour. As. Soc., Beng.*, XXII, 667.

[27] See G.O., No. 2069, 5th Sept. 1885; also *Ch. Coll. Magazine*, Madras, Vol. III. (No. 5, Nov. 1885), p. 377.

[28] Foulkes: *Ind. Antiq.*, VIII, 280.

carried on between the two. Asôka (260–223 B.C.), and Chandragupta (of the Mauriya Dynasty, B.C. 325–188) formed alliances with Antrochus, Antyonus, Ptolemy Philadelphus, and Magas of Cyrene, for the establishment of hospitals, and the protection of his co-religionists in their countries.[29] A much earlier intercourse is known to have existed between India, Egypt and other countries, but at so remote a period, that it could have had no effect on the present stone architecture of India, which, in fact, as far as is known, had no existence at that period. I may therefore only note it in passing. We read that "Thothmes III (? 1500 B.C.) "penetrated to the country of elephants."[30] The Hindus—though an ancient nation, had—before they were brought under European influence—no stone architecture. Any buildings they had, were—like those of the Burmese, and other eastern nations at the present day—constructed of wood. Their earliest stone examples show considerable traces of wooden construction still retained and applied in stone.

The Pandyans also, had communication with the Romans in the days of Augustus (27 B.C.); and there are records of a Hindu king having sent ambassadors to the Court of the Emperor.[31] The contemporary Chôḷa kingdom was known to the Greeks, and is mentioned in the *Periplus Maris Erithrœi* (A.D. 246–7) and in Ptolemy (A.D. 130).[32]

Whether a western colony ever settled on the east coast of Southern India, we have at present, no means of shewing. On the western Cochin coast at least, there was a temple of Augustus, and a garrison of soldiers at Muziris, (doubtfully) identified with Muyirikôḍu or Cranganore.[33]

Some evidences there are in the architecture also, which show more than a chance similarity in some points between that of the East and the West; forms which, although familiar enough to us in classical architecture, are found reproduced with modifications—suited to the position in which we find them—in Pallava architecture, showing that the one nation had probably been influenced in this art by the other.

The earliest notices speak of these people as Buddhists; and, in common with the change in religion, which was general over India, or through the personal leanings of individual sovereigns, we find the Jain, Śaivite, and Vaishnavite creeds being successively adopted as the religion of the people. In an extensive and populous country, changes in religious beliefs, so widely divergent in creed as these,—to be general,—must of necessity be gradual, and occupy many decades of time. We find Buddhists from Benares settling near Kâñchîpuram in the third century A.D.[34] But though the first Brahminic element appeared in the country at the end of the third century A.D., under Mukunti Pallava[35] it is not till the eighth century that we hear of the Buddhists' final expulsion from the city by Hêmaśîtaḷa.[36] About the time of Mukunti, it is said the Pallava written character was introduced into the kingdom.[37] This conflict of Brahmanism, in the Pallava country, with the prevailing religion—Buddhism, which it eventually overthrew—seems to have been a symptom of a great change which began to show itself at this period, over the whole of the Peninsula.[38]

---

[29] See Fergusson's *Ind. and Eas. Arch.*, pp. 17, 18, also p. 29, f. n, 2.

[30] See Brugsch (*Histoire d'Egypte*), I, p. 81. Burnell: *S.I. Palæ.*, p. 3.

[31] Wilson: *Catl. Mack. Coll.*, p. 44.

[32] *Ind. Antiq.*, VIII, 107, 331, 334, 337.

[33] Caldwell: *Drav. Gram*......*As. Res.*, X, 106.

[34] Wilson: *Catl. Mac. MSS.* 1. p. 1, XV, 1, XXVII. Rice. *Mys. Ins.*, p. 1, XXXVIII. Foulkes: *Sal. Manl.* I, 6, 10.

[35] Rice: *Mys. Ins.*, p. 1 XXXVIII.

[36] Wilson: *Catl. Mac. MSS.*, 1. p. 1, XV, 1, XVII; Taylor: *Jour. As. Soc., Beng.*, VII (II) 121; VIII, 284. Rice: *Mys. Ins.* p. 1 III, 1 VI.

[37] Burnell: *S.I. Palæ.*, 35, 36; Fleet: *Ind. Antiq.*, IX, 100. Princep: *Jour. As. Soc., Beng.*, III, 113, 119.

[38] Fergusson: *Ind. and Eas. Arch.*, pp. 21, 22.

In the fourth century, Vedenūr in Maisur, was part of the Pallava dominions,[39] and Trilochana reigned in the Dekkan.[40] In the same century, Fa Hian's five storeyed Po-lo-ye *Vihâra* was in existence.[41] About the end of this century, Trinêtra Pallava introduced other Brahmans into the country.[42] At this time, the Pallavas seem to have been at the zenith of their power, extending their sway over a large tract of territory. Their dominions are said to have extended along the eastern coast from Orissa to the mouth of the Southern Pennâr; inland, along the eastern boundary of the Koṅgu Karnata kingdom; and across the Tuṅgabhadrâ north-westwards, far into the northern Dekkan.[43] In confirmation of this, we read that at this time they were in the height of their power there;[44] and that previous to the arrival of the Châlukyans—who first established themselves in the Peninsula about the fifth century A.D.—the Pallavas were the dominant race in the Southern Dekkan.[45] But shortly after, they were engaged in a series of struggles,—principally with the Châlukyans—and by the middle of the fifth century, we have the record of their first defeat by—a comparatively insignificant power—the Kadambas.[46] Their power, from this epoch, seemed to have declined, for their history from this time onwards—which is more continuously recorded than that of the centuries preceding it—is simply a succession of struggles and defeats by neighbouring powers, varied by gleams of flickering success. As their rise had been gradual, so was their decline, not the work of a single blow, but a continuous sapping away of their strength by petty struggles. We have numerous records of the capture, and destruction by fire, of their capital city Kâñchîpuram; first by Pulikêsi I. (Châlukyan) in the beginning of the sixth century;[47] and later, we hear, of the desolation of the town by invading armies; but these could only have been partial. It always managed to resuscitate itself, and even now, it remains one of the largest and most flourishing towns in Southern India. Other invaders were so struck by the beauties of its architectural works, that instead of destroying them, they took means for their perpetuation. An early inscription at the Kailâsanâdha temple[48] records that Vikramâditya actually visited the temple, and who, influenced probably by religious feeling, left the temple intact, and perpetuated the memory of his capture by this inscription. This is the most probable way of explaining the existence of this early and important Châlukyan record. He, and other kings of the same dynasty acted similarly. Vikramâditya II. (733–750) A.D. "determined to root out the Pallavas, the obscurers of "the splendour of the former kings of his line, and by nature hostile, going with great "speed into the Udâka province, slew in battle the Pallava named Nandi-Pôtavarma who "came against him, captured his defiant lotus-mouthed trumpet, his drum called 'Roar of the "sea,' his chariot, his standard, immense and celebrated elephants, clusters of rubies, which "by their radiance dispelled all darkness; and entering Kâñchîpuram—the Zone (Kâñchî) "as it were of the lady, the region of Agastya's abode (the south), acquired the great merit "of covering with gold Râja Simhêśvara, and other Dêvakala sculptured in stone, which "Narasimha Pôta-Varmâ, the protector of indigent Brahmans. . . . . . . had made."

---

[39] Rice: *Mys. Ins.*, p. 1 III, 1. IV.

[40] Elliot: *Madr. Jour. Lit. and Sci.*, XX, 78. Rice: *Mys. Ins.*, p. 1 III, 1 IV. *Ind. Antiq.*, II, 156, VIII, 246. Fleet: *Ind. Antiq.*, VII, 243, 245. *Kan. Dyn.*, 19.

[41] Remusat: Fa Hian, 314. Cunningham: *Anc. Geo. Ind.*, I, 522. Fergusson and Burgess *Cave. Tem.*, 129. See Burgess; *Report, S. Ind.*, Vol. I.

[42] Wilson: *Catl. Mac.* MSS., I, p. CXX. Fleet: *Ind. Antiq.*, VII, 246. Foulkes: *Sal. Man.*, I, 10.

[43] Foulkes: *Ind. Antiq.*, VI, 22. Sewell: *Jour. R.A.S.*, XVI (N.S.), 31. [44] Foulkes: *Ind. Antiq.*, VIII, 172.

[45] Burgess: *Arch. Rep. W. Ind. Bidar*, 23. Fleet: *Ind. Antiq.*, V, 50. Rice; *Ind. Antiq.*, II, 156. Elliot: *Jour. R.A.S.*, I (N.S.), 251.

[46] Fleet: *Ind. Antiq.*, VI, 22, *Dyn.*, 9. [47] Burgess: *Arch. Rep.* Bidar., 25 Fleet· *Kan. Dyn.* 2

[48] *South Ind. Ins.*, Vol. IX, p. 147.

In connection with the covering of the statues with gold, an inscription in the Kailâsanâdha temple mentions a similar act, and I am inclined to believe, probably refers to the same instance as the above. If so, it may prove of great importance in fixing the date of the building. It is somewhat fragmentary, but it records the giving of some grain, and gold, the latter being for ornamenting ". . . . . Sudêvar;" which evidently coincides with the "other Dêva kala" mentioned above. Should this be so, and the inscription of Vikramâditya refer to the sculptures in this temple, then the clearly stated fact that they were made by Narasimha Pôta-Varmâ should fix the date of their execution during his reign, about the end of the sixth century.[50] But as all the sculptures of this temple have evidently been executed after the construction of the building, and when each stone was in its fixed position, the actual foundation of the structure should be placed earlier. Few or any of the sculptures are cut out of a single stone, the joints of the masonry go right through them, and they could not possibly have been executed before they were set in position. Fergusson also mentions[51] that this custom is usual in India where the buildings "are always set up in block, and the carving executed *in situ*." Considering the dates assigned to the Mâmallâpuram works, and the architectural features of the Kailâsanâdha temple, which would lead us to place it earlier than these, the inference drawn from the above historical facts may not be far amiss. Briefly stated, the presumptive evidences in favour of the above theory, are,—the architecture of the building seems to point to a period coinciding with that referred to in the inscription of Vikramâditya;—the "Dêva kala" would most probably be in some temple or other. This temple of Kailâsanâdha would, in early times, be a most important and sacred shrine, the immense amount of sculpture and labour spent on it, points to this. An inscription in it[52] refers to it as "this temple of stone called Râjasimhêśvara, which touches the clouds with its top, which robs Kailâsa of its beauty." Then there is the inscription in the temple itself—recording a similar act—and another by Vikramâditya, on a pier of the *Mahâmaṇḍapam*, proving that he *did* make a grant to this temple; and moreover, some of the sculptures themselves countenance the fact, as several have jewel holes in the ears, evidently intended for the attachment of some sort of metal ornament.

In the sixth century, the Pallavas still ruled the Vengi country;[53] and Badami was temporarily recovered by them.[54] Mrigêsa built a Jain temple at Palâsikâ;[55] and in the first quarter of the same century, an ambassador from Southern India—possibly from the Pallava Court—visited China,[56] showing that they still retained their position among the nations.

Râjêndra-Varmâ was possibly reigning at the beginning of this century, succeeded by Vishṇu-Simha or Nara-Simha Varma who probably reigned about the end of the century, for we have the record of his death in battle at the beginning of the seventh.[57] The latter is seemingly the king of the same name mentioned, as having caused the execution of the sculptures noted above. They suffered shortly after this, several crushing defeats from the

---

[49] Rice: *Ind. Antiq.*, VIII, 24, 28. *Mys. Ins.*, 300. *S.I. Ins.*, IX, p. 146. See further remarks under description of the sculptures.

[50] See Fleet: *Ind. Antiq.*, IX, 99. *Kan. Dyn.*, 16. Foulkes: *R.A.S.G.B.*, Vol. XVII, part 2 (the Pallavas), p. 10.

[51] *Ind. and Eas. Arch.*, p. 339.

[52] *South. Ind. Ins.*, IX, 14.

[53] Rice: *Mys. Ins*, p. 1, III. Eggling: *Ind. Antiq.*, III, 152.

[54] Fleet: *Ind. Antiq.*, IX, 100.

[55] Fleet: *Kan. Dyn*, 15. Buhler: *Ind. Antiq.*, VI, 31.

[56] *Jour., As. Soc., Beng.*, VI, 66. *Ind. Antiq.*, IX, 16, 17. *Jour., R.A.S.*, VI, 468.

[57] Eggling: *Ind. Antiq.*, iii, 152. Fleet: *Ind. Antiq.*, VI, 78, IX, 99. *Kan. Dyn.*, 16. Rice: *Mys. Ins.*, p. 1, iii. Foulkes *J.R.A.S.*, Vol. XVII, part 2 (the Pallavas), p. 10.

Châlukyans; and Vikramâditya I. "forced the King of Kâñchîpuram, who had never bowed down to any man, to lay his crown at his feet."[58] A king of this race, however, still reigned in Kalinga, and some victories over the Châlukyans are recorded.[59] But in the beginning of the seventh century, Vikramâditya, "with irresistible might, subdued the Pallava country and made the lord of Kâñchîpuram kiss his lotus feet."[60] The Veṅgi Pallavas were conquered about the same time,[61] and they seem generally to have been hard pressed by their enemies on all sides. They were defeated and "ruined" by a western Châlukyan (Satyâśraya) and driven behind the walls of Kâñchîpuram.[62] Narasiṁha Pôta Varma was defeated and trodden to death by elephants.[63] A temporary truce seems, however, to have been concluded between the two powers; for, although the Châlukyans had generally been the victors, they would no doubt suffer heavily in their struggles with such a powerful foe. We thereafter find the Pallava Chaṇḍadaṇḍa in alliance with Pulikêsi II. (Châlukyan); and the Pallavas still reigning at Kâñchîpuram[64] when Hieun Thsang visited the city, which was at this time, six miles long. Its inhabitants were brave, just, learned, pious and tolerant in religion; and the then flourishing condition of the north-eastern districts is shewn by the numerous Buddhist monasteries and Hindu temples he found throughout this portion of his route.[65] He found Buddhist buildings of great beauty at Dhanakataka;[66] and a richly sculptured monastery at Pingkila.[67] The truce with the Châlukyans seems to have been of no great duration, for we find after this, they received a succession of humiliating defeats from these and other minor powers up to the end of the ninth century. We then—for the first time—hear of the Chôḷas in connection with them; so that up to this period, and before the Chôḷas came into conflict with them, their former power must have been considerably shattered and broken. Their struggles with the other powers had so weakened them, that this new enemy could not be effectively resisted, and they finally fell before the rising Chôḷa power.

The Jains whom Hieun Thsang calls Nirgranthas, were numerous in the seventh century. The last Buddhist king, Hêmasitaḷa,[68] became a convert to the Jain religion, and drove the Buddhists from the capital. He is also said to have brought a large Jain colony from the north to Kâñchîpuram.[69] The last mention of the Pallavas, as a race or dynasty is in the thirteenth century A.D.,[70] though after the conquest of Toṇḍamaṇḍala by the Râjas of Vijayanagar, some of the Kurumbar chieftains regained influence, and still held forts there, as late as the sixteenth century.[71] The Pallavas—as a dynasty—had completely disappeared, and the city of Kâñchîpuram, afterwards passed through various vicissitudes. In this sketch, only leading points in their history have been touched on; but the materials are only sufficient to give a faint outline of what this people must have been: letting us know that the Pallavas, during their possession of power, and, even long after their decline had begun, were one of the most prominent ruling races in the Southern Peninsula.

---

[58] Rice: *Ind. Antiq.*, VIII, 24. [59] Fleet: *Ind. Antiq.*, X, 243. Foulkes: *Ind. Antiq.*, VIII, 277, 281.

[60] Elliot: *Jour. R.A.S.*, IV, 10. Bhagavanlal Indraji: *Jour. As. Soc., Beng.*, XVI, 4, 6.

[61] Burgess: *Arch. Rep.*, Bidar., 26. Fleet: *Dyn.* 15, 23. [62] Fleet: *Ind. Antiq.*, V, 67, 73, *Dyn.*, 24.

[63] Fleet: *Ind. Antiq.*, VI, 78. Rice: *Mys. Ins.* p. x, 1, iii, I, iii, I, V, 1, XII.

[64] Fergusson and Burgess: *Cave. Tem.*, 108. Fleet: *Ind. Antiq.*, VIII, 245.

[65] Julien: *Mémoires* II, 118. Beal's *Bud. Rec.*, W., World II, 229.

[66] Cunningham: *Anc. Geo. Ind.* I, 540.

[67] Julien: II. 106; Burnell: *S.I. Palæ.*, 16. Foulkes: *Salem Manl.*, I, 9.

[68] Taylor: *Madr. Jour., Lit. and Sci.*, VII, 20, 219; VIII, 261.

[69] Wilson: *Catl. Mac.* MSS., 1, p. 1, XV., 1, XVII. Taylor: *Jour., As. Soc., Beng.*, VII (II), 110. 121. VII, 284. *Madr. Jour., Lit. and Sci.*, VII, 8. Rice: *Mys. Ins.*, p. 1, III, I, VI.

[70] Burnell: *S.I. Palæ.*, 36. Sewell: *Lists* I, 177.

[71] Taylor: *Jour., As. Soc., Beng.*, VII (II). *Madr. Jour., Lit. and Sci.*, VII, 321.

PALLAVA ARCHITECTURE.

In treating of their architecture, it is almost unnecessary to remark that the people who excavated the works at Mâmallâpuram,—whose date has been assigned to about the sixth century A.D.,[72] had evidently—even at that early date—a very complete knowledge of the art. But, these monolithic works are only imitations of structural works previously existing, either in their own, or neighbouring countries. That many such, did at one time exist in the Pallava country is more than probable; and Kâñchîpuram is undoubtedly the place where we would expect to find the earliest buildings, for Mâmallâpuram and Sâlavankuppam were only the seaports of the capital city, and therefore likely to be of more modern date than the metropolis itself. During the many invasions suffered by Kâñchîpuram, most of the ancient buildings and sculptures would doubtless suffer, or be completely destroyed; for, of the Pallava buildings remaining, only six have as yet been brought to notice. No complete structural examples of the works of this dynasty have been found in any other place in the Chingleput District, with the exception of the temples at Kûram, Tiruppadikuṉram and those on the coast, at Mâmallâpuram. The Kûram temple is not of pure Pallava architecture, and should be classed under the transitional period between the Pallava and Chôḷa styles. These two temples of Kûram and Tiruppadikuṉram have none of the sculptures peculiar to the other examples noted. The copperplate *sasanam* belonging to the Kûram temple would seem to show that although the shrine is now devoted to the worship of Vishṇu, it was originally consecrated to Śiva.[73] Although we have found no other complete examples of Pallava buildings, many *yâḷi* pillars and other fragments are still to be seen scattered about Kâñchîpuram and in villages in the district, which are evidently the remains of former buildings of this style.[74]

The other early temples in Kâñchîpuram are the work of the Chôḷas; and however interesting they may be as the works of that race, they are decidedly less important archæologically than the earlier Pallava buildings.

From every point of view, the most important of the group of Pallava structures is the Kailâsanâdha temple, which is one of the most remarkable architectural monuments in the district, alike for the extent and beauty of its sculptures—forming a complete series of representations of the principal legends in the Śaivite mythology—and from the fact that its architectural features when compared with those of the *rathas* at Mâmallâpuram, show an

---

[72] Fergusson: *Hist. Ind. and Eas. Arch.*, 326. Fergusson and Burgess: Cave Temples. *Madras Jour.*, XIII (i), 53.

[73] *South Ind. Ins.*, Vol. IX, p. 144.

[74] The temple at Maṇimangalam has been thought by Mr. Sewell to be of very ancient date.* The statement, that "the *gôpura* is apsidal ended" is not quite correct—the back of the shrine, and the greater portion of the tower over it, are square; but the upper portion of the *vimâna* tower, or, more properly, the *śikara* only, has a circular back. The temple itself, is a Chôḷa structure of the eleventh century. More characteristic examples of the peculiarity referred to (*i.e.*, semi-circular ended shrines) are seen at different places in the district; and it seems to have been—from the number I have observed—quite a usual feature in Chôḷa temples. Somangalam, Tennêri, Mâgaralu, and Tiruppadikuṉram Jain temple, afford examples of this circular-ended *vimâna* (*Gajaprishthakriti Garbhagraham*;—or elephant back shaped shrine). These are however, all of Chôḷa date. There is a likelihood of some or all of them having been modelled *from* the "*Sahâdêva*" *ratha* at Mâmallâpuram, but by no possibility could any of them have supplied the model for its design. Of an oval shaped shrine, the Chôḷa temple of *Iravatânêśvara* at Kâñchîpuram, is a good specimen.

* *Lists of Antiq.*, I, p. 187, and II, p. 255.

I would here point out, that the names applied to the *rathas* at Mâmallâpuram must be modern, and cannot be the original appellations of these temples. The names are those of the five Pândavas, and are given to them by the present natives of the village. As elsewhere in India, the villagers assign every ancient building, or excavation of which the origin is unknown, to the Jains, or to such personages as Râma,† and the five Pândavas. In some districts, they ascribe to the Chôḷas, buildings which have not the slightest connection with them, but simply through the tradition—having been handed down—that the Chôḷas were the builders of great works. The term "shore" temple applied to the building on the coast at Mâmallâpuram, also seems to me to be a corruption of the word "Chôḷa" temple. The natives, when asked the name of the building, call it the "Chôḷa *Kôil*," and this might easily be misunderstood by Europeans unacquainted with the word—for the similarly sounding word "shore;" more especially as it actually is on the seashore, and part of it, in the sea itself.

† See also Burnell: *S. I. Palæ.* p. VII.

earlier period in the Pallava style common to both. So also is it with regard to the other Pallava temples in Kâñchîpuram. The inscriptions in it are numerous, and mostly in an early palæographical form of the Pallava Grantha character, similar to others at Mâmallâpuram. The names on the niches here, are the same as those on the Dharmarâja's *Ratha* at Mâmallâpuram with others in addition; and, the king's name we find there, also occurs here.[75] A notable peculiarity is the scrolled foliation attached to letters of the inscriptions in front of the cells in the courtyard. They are similar in this respect, to some of the earlier Châlukyan inscriptions in the north. They are identical palæographically, with the Nâgarî inscription at Sâlavankuppam. A Châlukyan grant on one of the piers of the *mahâmaṇḍapam* by "Vikramâditya Satyâśraya Śrî Prithivîvallabha" is interesting as proving one of the Châlukyan invasions of Kâñchîpuram; and is an important link in the chain of evidence pointing to the early date to which we must assign this structure.[76] The inscriptions at the other Pallava temples are in Tamil, and of a much later date than those at the Kailâsanâdha temple.

The massive piers in the Kailâsanâdha *mahâmaṇḍapam* also indicate an early period of the style. They are placed at a distance of two and-a-half diameters from each other. This peculiar solidity in the supports is found in all early examples of every style of architecture,—Classical, Gothic and others; and if a comparison be made between these piers and the widely-spaced slender columns of the adjoining *ardhamaṇḍapam*—a Vijayanagar structure, which has been built on the vacant space which, in the original design separated the *mahâmaṇḍapam* from the *vimâna* itself,[77]—or the *yâli* piers of the other Pallava temples, it will show clearly that this building should rank as an early example of an early period in the Pallava style (Plates Nos. XLVIII (Fig. 1), XXXIX (Fig. 2), XCVIII, XCIX, LXXXVII).

The piers have a striking resemblance to those used in early cave temples; and, as only the more slender, and obviously later ornamental *yâli* piers are used at the "Dharmarâjâ's" and other *rathas*, and caves at Mâmallâpuram, this feature may, in conjunction with other architectural evidences, warrant us in assigning this building to fully as early a date as any of the Pallava works yet known.

Considering the large amount of sculpture there is in these temples generally, and in the Kailâsanâdha in particular, the general excellence which characterizes it throughout, is very striking.

The animals sculptured as supports in Pallava architecture are always lions, and never tigers. Burnell has, from one doubtful example on a seal[78] given the emblem of the Pallavas as a tiger. This seems without doubt to be erroneous. In not a single known Pallava building is a tiger represented: on the other hand, lions are always sculptured in

---

[75] *South Ind. Ins.*, Vol. IX, pp. 1–12.

[76] *Epigraphia Indica*, Vol. III, part VIII, p. 369.

[77] During the excavations which I conducted in 1884 at the "shore" temple at Mâmallâpuram, this feature of design in that building was also found, *i.e.*, a shrine with lofty tower over it, a vacant space in front; and a detached *maṇḍapam* was unearthed. At the Kaliâsanâdha temple, the space between the once detached shrine and *mahâmaṇḍapam*, has been filled in with a comparatively recent *arddhamaṇḍapam*, to suit the modern requirements of worship in the temple. This is proved by the style of the addition itself, and the fact that the ancient Pallava Grantha inscriptions returning along the back of the base of the originally detached *maṇḍapam*, and along the front base of the large vimâna, as well as some sculptures, are abutted against by the walls of the more recent building.*

* See also *Epigraphia Indica*, Vol. III, part VIII, p. 359.

This arrangement of a detached *maṇḍapam* seems to have been not unusual in early times, for in addition to the examples noted, another well-known specimen at Mâmallâpuram—shows the same grouping; I refer to the monolithic works known as "*Bhima's*," and "*Dharmarâjâ's*" *rathas*. *Dharmarâjâ's* has a *vihâra* roof, *Bhimâ's*, though a hall, has a high tower, and *Dharmarâjâ's* is the smaller in plan and nearly square, while the other is long. These stand almost in a line with each other. The first—from its design—was probably intended to be the temple, or shrine; and the other, the *mahâmaṇḍapam*. In the treatment of the lower storey, this latter is formed on the same design as the *mahâmaṇḍapam* at the Kailâsanâdha temple;—that is, with the open pillared spaces on each façade, and the return walls, with panels, at each corner. These Mâmallâpuram *rathas* stand north and south, but this is not quite exceptional; and in this case the natural arrangement of the rocks out of which they are cut, must have decided this.

[78] *S. Ind. Palæ.*, p. 106 and plate.

different positions and places on their shrines, presumably because it was the emblem of a king or kings of the dynasty. The lions at these Kâñchîpuram temples, at the *rathas* and caves at Mâmallâpuram are sufficiently numerous to support the theory. A close observation of the so-called "tiger cave," at Salavankuppam, will show that the "tigers" there, are a complete misnomer, the sculptures undoubtedly represent lions. Beads and coins found at Mâmallâpuram show a distinct lion on one side and an elephant on the other. The dynastic crest, is said to have been a bull.[79]

The application of human figures, or caryatides, as supports, is seen on the bases of two piers inserted in the Kachchêśvara temple, and on another complete pier in a *maṇḍapam* in *Sengaḷanîr Ódai* street, (Plates Nos. XXI, XXII).

These latter have been said to be representations of the old Kurumbar inhabitants,[80] but the term "Kurumbar" was a name bestowed on the Pallava people generally, and they would probably not care intentionally to represent themselves in this servile position. In the Classical Caryatides, it was only the conquered races who were thus shown in sculpture, not the conquerors, to whom the sculptors themselves belonged. Possibly these are representations of the Kondaikatti Villâlars, or of some other tribe originally settled in the country, and likely to be in subjection to the Pallavas.

This tribe was so named,[81] from their tying the hair in a tuft on the crown of the head, instead of leaving a small lock (*kudumi*)[82] behind, as worn in most parts of India; or in front, as worn in Malayâlam. It will be seen that this mode, peculiar to the Villâlars, is clearly reproduced on the figures of these pillars, and would distinctly point to their being representations of this tribe. What is shown, is a group of figures ranged round a pier, and acting as supporters. The application is even closer than the *yâḷi* in its similarity to the Caryatides. The *gandharva* supporting figures in the bases and cornices of Pallava architecture also illustrate the same idea. The simultaneous use of this feature in the two styles is worthy of note; and, granted the possibility of its showing that intercourse had taken place between the Greeks and Pallavas, the probability is, that, unless examples of this feature are found in India of a date anterior to that at which we find the Greeks using it—which is very unlikely—we may assume that some of the Indians who visited the West in early times, had brought the idea back with them. That there is certainly more than mere supposition in this theory, is seen by the prevalence—although slightly in the Pallava style—very commonly in later works, of debased applications of classical moulded and ornamental features.[83]

---

[79] *Epigraphia Indica*, Vol. IV, Part IV, p. 177.

[80] Sewell; *Lists* II, p. 264, and *Jour., R.A.S.*, Vol. XVI, Part I, p. 6.

[81] Wilson: *Catl. Mac. Colln.*, p. 204; also F.N. 6., p. 6, (*Ib.*).

[82] *Ind Ant*, IV., 166 F, on the Kudumi.

[83] In other parts of India, western influence shows itself in the architectural arts. The rails at Buddh Gaya, and Bharut (B.C. 250-200), from the distinct classical individuality of their sculptures, mark this clearly. But whether this arose through a school of sculpture having been imported from the Baktrian Greeks, or through intercourse maintained with Rome and Byzantium during the early centuries, is not quite clear, probably both influences were at work.* This influence reached its culminating point in the sculptures at Amarâvati, which partake of both the characteristics of the East and West. Their Western tendency is, I should be inclined to think, allied more to the Greek than the Roman school. If this influence showed itself so markedly at an early period, it is not unreasonable to suppose it might appear in other forms, the more so, as the early Pallavas had intercourse with the Baktrians and Romans also. Any buildings that may have existed in India before 250 B.C. were constructed of wood, and it was only after Alexander's raid, followed by the establishment of the Baktrian kingdom,—which latterly extended its influence to the Indus,—that the stone building of the West became general in the East. Its influence was thereafter felt on the coinage, sculpture, and arts generally.† These facts, taken collectively, tend to show how much the Eastern architectural arts owe in their development to those of the West. Although this impulse, to the construction of buildings in stone, is clearly traceable to Western influence, yet the early Indian architects by no means slavishly copied classical forms for their buildings. It is only in the details of parts that we see these appearing. The designs of the temples generally, are, with few exceptions, extremely striking in their individuality of conception, and arrangement of parts; and each and every province, though adopting forms found in other districts, worked out almost a distinctive style of its own. The great beauty of certain styles of Indian architecture consists in the originality and diversity, and yet continuity of forms which pervade them.

* Fergusson: *Ind. and Eas. Arch.*, p. 31.

† Fergusson: *Ind. and Eas. Arch.*, p. 48.

The bold application of the lion support, is peculiar to this style only. It is not used to any great extent in later Dravidian examples; and, even when we find evidences of it appearing, it has lost entirely the significance of its early use. Representations of elephants are—in a way—commonly used as supports, or rather bearers, and with the lion (*yâli*), are about the only animals I have observed, used as such (Plate No. XXIII, Figs. 1, 2, 3). Other instances of the application—at various places in India—of figures used as supports, might be multiplied indefinitely,—a pillar at Barôli is an example[84]. But what has already been said is sufficient to show that this, along with many other architectural features, has analogies in Classical styles. Later Dravidian works have, in their base mouldings, and inferior cornices generally, corrupt imitations of Classical details and ornament. In the latter, the bead and reel, and egg and dart ornaments are conspicuous; but—as characteristic of their designs generally—applied without the discrimination by which they should be guided in using the different forms of details. These mouldings increase their resemblance in some points as the style advances, and in a few instances so does the general design of the building.[85] It would be interesting to trace the origin of the late Dravidian heavy over-hanging cornice which in its general outline is exactly the reverse of the classical.

As to this feature, it has been remarked[86] by Fergusson that "it seems impossible that" ". . . . the great cornice of double curvature could have been brought to these fixed "forms without long experience, and the difficulty is to understand how they could ever "have been elaborated in stone at all, as they are so unlike lithic forms found anywhere "else; yet they are not wooden, nor is there any trace in them of any of their details being "derived from wooden architecture, as is so evidently the case with the Buddhist architec-"ture of the north. The one suggestion that occurs to me is that they are derived from "terra-cotta forms." In support of this theory it is remarked that, at the present day, large figures of horsemen, and giants on foot,—made of a terra-cotta substance—are found near some village temples; as also that the figures on *gôpurams* are not—as sometimes stated—always made of plaster, but are often formed of burnt clay. This theory holds good as regards the figures, but no examples so far as is known, are found of terra-cotta being applied to cornices. A more probable origin of the heavy cornice is found in large flat sloping slabs which are seen to serve the purpose in some of the earlier Châlukyan temples.[87] This form presents a number of serious defects in construction, to obviate which, the curved cornice seems to have been designed, for we find it invariably occurring in later Châlukyan examples. First, the early slab cornice, gives the desired shade, but the greater portion of it projects over the wall, giving a very minimum of stability. Secondly, it does not lie on a flat bed, and is therefore liable to slide off the wall: and thirdly, there is a difficulty in getting a proper rest for the stone beams and slabs of the flat roof. It has, in certain cases, been attempted to correct this, by pillar supports at the outer edge. The curved form obviates all these; its upper portion—which rests on the wall,—being flat; and, though the bulk of the cornice still projects over the wall, it can be, and

---

[84] See Fergusson: *Ind. and East Arch.*, p. 451, pp. 1-251.

[85] The *Ganêśa* temple near Hampi, for example, has the large cell in which sits the god with a colonnade of lofty bracketed columns in front. This portico—from a short distance—has exactly the general appearance of an Ionic temple, *minus* the raking pediment over the façade. This of course is only in the general effect, the details bear no resemblance.

[86] *History of Indian and Eastern Architecture*, p. 373.

[87] See New Imperial Series—*Archæological Survey of India*, Vol. XXI., Pl. III., figs. 1 and 3.

is prevented from overbalancing, by masonry resting on the top, which restores the equilibrium. In the Dravidian temples, a further safeguard was added, by a small beam running parallel to, and resting on brackets projecting from the wall. This beam supported the slabs of the cornice at about the middle of the under side of the curve, and, to get a proper rest, the under side had a number of wide hollow flutes added, one of which, rested on the beam.

The bold overhanging cyma reversa cornice of late structures, is not found in the early Pallava style as represented at Kâñchîpuram and Mâmallâpuram. At the latter place however, it is slighty more marked than at the former. In some of the Elurâ rock cuttings, we find a striking similarity in general effect and detail with these Kâñchîpuram works. At Elurâ however, we have an approach to the heavy cornice referred to. It is evidently an advance in the period of art which seems—to a certain extent—to be common to all; and, unless the style at these northern examples advanced more rapidly than in the South, it would be evidence in favour of placing the southern temples earlier than the others. Another prominent and striking similarity between the Kâñchîpuram Kailâsanâdha and Vaikuṇṭha Perumâl temples, the Kailâsanâdha temple at Elurâ, and temples at Mâmallâpuram, is the peculiar form of the octagonal *śikhara* of the towers; they are almost identical in each case; and, as this feature, in a form so markedly distinct, is not found later on, it would show that there must have been a very close connection between the builders of all the three groups.[88] The close affinity between the architecture of Elurâ, and that of Mâmallâpuram has been elsewhere noted, and the inferences given, for the supposition that the architects of the latter were the Châlukyans. The most obvious inference which ought to be drawn is, that as Elurâ is clearly later than either Mâmallâpuram, or the best examples at Kâñchîpuram, the builders of Elurâ came from the south, and not the Mâmallâpuram sculptors from the North. The pure Châlukyan style is entirely different from the Pallava, and although southern features are not wanting in Châlukyan works, such as do occur, are evidently foreign to the general characteristics of the style. Few of the features of Pallava architecture have any resemblance whatever to the leading characteristics of Châlukyan art The only details I have seen at Kâñchîpuram, bearing a faint resemblance to Châlukyan sculptures, are the perforated windows and accessory panels at the Kachchêśvara and Kailâsanâdha temples; but any similarity they may have, could only have resulted through an attempt at imitation by Pallava workmen. The finding of a few solitary examples of a southern style in a northern province,—with a distinct style of its own—is no proof that those in the North executed them. If this style is proved to be peculiar to, and general in parts of the South, then the resultant inference is that the southern people were the designers or workmen. If Châlukyan architects or workmen had produced the Elurâ or Mâmallâpuram rock cuttings, we should have had, not examples of pure Pallava art,—though probably a rude imitation of it,—but most certainly Châlukyan designs pure and simple. The architectural evidence proves that the architects were, not the Châlukyans, but the Pallavas themselves.[89] Another northern temple—that at Paṭṭadakal—shows some architectural features in common with those at Kâñchîpuram. It was "built by Vikramâditya's queen, expressly to celebrate another victory over the King of Kâñchîpuram." (733 Cir.)[90] It is most probable that Pallava workers were taken north to aid in its construction. The king, from inscriptional

---

[88] See also Burgess: *Arch. Rep. W. Ind.*, 1877-80, Pl. I; and Fergusson: *Ind. and East Arch.*, p. 328.

[89] See also Fergusson and Burgess: *Cave temples*, 139, 140.

[90] Fleet: *Ind. Antiq.*, VI, 85, X, 163, 164, 165.

evidence, seems to have been impressed with the beauty of the architecture he saw at Kâñchîpuram, and may have desired to have reproductions in his own dominions.

The two shrines of Tripurântakêśvara and Airâvatêśvara are small structures, with their sculptures much weatherworn, and filled in, in some cases, with brickwork and plaster. Scenes similar to those at the other examples are however, represented in the sculptures, and the kind of stone itself, general effect, and character of the different parts are sufficient to classify them.

Tradition relates that two pillars standing erect in the road leading west from the Varadarâja temple, are the piers of the gateway to the ancient fortified city.[91] Another of a similar kind is seen lying on the ground in front of the Vaikuṇtha Perumâḷ temple. The first two, *may* have formed the gateway of any walls there might have been during the fifteenth century,—though even for this, they are too slender and widely spaced,—but they could not by any possibility, have served a similar purpose during the Pallava occupation: the piers are of Vijayanagar design. (See Figs. 5 and 6, Plate No. LII.)

Before describing each of the structures in detail, it will be advisable to make a few further remarks on the leading features of this style and its relation to later Dravidian architecture, of which it is one of the chief forerunners.

There is an unmistakably characteristic individuality common to Pallava monolithic and structural temples, which at once singles them out from—and can in no wise lead to their being associated with—the mass of later Dravidian works. The later forms, though striking enough examples of a development of this primary style,—modified according to the periods to which they actually belong,—are yet, by the very exuberance of crowded detail, and want of architectural effect which characterize Dravidian architecture generally, sufficient to produce a result almost as striking as that between two distinct styles. In the Pallava—though there is abundance of detail and sculpture—the design has been so well thought out, and systematically expressed in stone, as to get the very architectural effect which the later architecture lacks. This is, to a great extent, accomplished by the application of the true principles of design; in the grouping of a number of minor features round about,—and leading the eye up to—the central and crowning object of the structure; in these cases, this is the *vimâna* tower. The Kailâsanâdha is an example of this principle applied with good effect. The central object is the great tower over the shrine, with lesser towers over the shrines at each of its corners and at the centre of each face. The view outside would originally be extremely effective, for, in the peculiar arrangement of cells grouped along each side of the courtyard, each shrine has a small tower over it, which stood clear of the courtyard wall head. The modern owners of the building have, however, done their best to spoil the effect, by filling in the spaces between the spires with masonry, so that the minarets are completely blocked up; and the outer faces of the courtyard present only a continuous line of wall, without varied skyline.[92] That the original builders had a knowledge of the right application of materials for sound construction, is seen by the fact, that, though the temples are built of a soft sandstone, admitting of great facilities for the execution of sculpture—the sub-basements and plinths supporting the piers and walls of the superstructure are all of granite. These are the points bearing the greatest superincumbent weight, or where fracture or decay would be most likely to affect the stability of the building.

91 Sewell: *Lists*, II, p. 205.

92 In a recent restoration of the temple, these blocking walls have been removed

Fergusson points out [53] the want of true architectural effect which characterizes Dravidian architecture as a whole; where the principal objects are on the outside of the design, and there is no central feature. This is evidently caused by the later architects misunderstanding or not thoroughly appreciating the principles by which they should be guided in forming the outline features of their designs. A want of appreciation of this fact is a radical defect, which the application of any amount of laborious detail can in no wise remedy; and the only effect obtained, is to give the feeling that all the work is so much labour lost, or applied to little or no purpose, and that a better architectural effect might be had with half the toil there mis-spent.

In addition to the faultiness of Dravidian designs, the several component features are always covered with a multiplicity of crowded detail or ornament. This does nothing to enhance the design viewed at any distance, and the only feeling produced, is one of wonder at the amount of patience the workers must have had to execute it. This detail is often minutely cut, and, on columns, and in interiors,—where it is intended to be, and can only be seen from a short distance,—has a striking effect; but, on *gôpurams*, and other portions of the buildings—far removed from the eye—all this minute detail is of little use in producing the desired result. That the true principle can be applied,—and that with good effect—to Dravidian architecture, these Pallava temples exemplify.

It may, however, be granted that this effect is much easier of attainment in a small, than in a large building, and that the structures under notice are,—compared with the huge areas covered by some of the prominent Dravidian temples,—relatively small. In the larger temples, a central object, so far removed from the eye of an outside observer, would probably require—to be effective—to be built to an altitude beyond the limits of expense and construction to which the builders could attain: but I would remark that this need not necessarily be the case; the *gôpurams* generally placed at the entrances are, in many cases, immense structures, striking the immediate beholder with their massiveness, and the degree of labour bestowed on them. A central tower, probably a little greater than each of these, with smaller towers over the gateways, need not be more expensive, or overtax the constructive abilities of the builders, and would prove an immeasurably more effective grouping as a whole, than the ineffective arrangement we generally see adopted in these large Dravidian temples. An example of this, is the temple at Tañjûr. It is however, comparatively early, being of Chôḷa date. It shews the application to a large temple, of such an arrangement as I have noted, and is a noteworthy specimen of this principle applied with stately effect. The early architects never lost sight of it, but later on, as the style advanced, this principle of design was entirely reversed, till what should have been the principal feature,—the central shrine tower—became in fact, the most diminutive object in the entire structure, almost or quite invisible from an outside standpoint.

There is one thing however, to be said in palliation of the faulty design seen in some of the larger temples. There were very few of them built at one consecutive time. Many were originally, groups of small shrines, latterly walled in to make one large temple; and, as each succeeding king made additions to the building, he strove to excel the works of his predecessor. The result was, that the principal features came to occupy the exterior portions of the structure. If a Dravidian architect had had an opportunity of constructing

[53] *Hist. Ind. and East Arch.*, pp. 347–350.

a large temple in its entirety, and from *one* pre-conceived design, he might probably have produced a work retaining in its features and their grouping, more of the spirit and true effect of good architecture, than those now ranked as typical examples of the style. But such is the effect of custom and long familiarity with forms—though avowedly wrong, and brought about by indirect means,—that if a large temple were ever to be built now-a-days, an Indian architect would, most probably as not, adopt *in extenso* the models he sees standing before him.

KAILÂSANÂDHA TEMPLE, KÂÑCHÎPURAM.

This building stands in the fields some distance to the west of the town, and a few hundred yards south-west of the great Śiva temple at Kâñchîpuram.

As mentioned in the foregoing introductory remarks, it is, among the group of Pallava temples, under notice, by far the most important.

For a South Indian temple, its plan is somewhat peculiar. It is unusual, only through comparison with the generally accepted arrangement seen in Dravidian Hindu temples; but these latter,—compared with this—are comparatively modern; and the length of time that has elapsed from the time of its building to the foundation of these others, has led to the modifications of plan adapted to modern requirements. The plan has undoubtedly been, not an unusual one for Hindu temples in early days; and similar buildings of a somewhat contemporary date,—as still exist—leave no doubt on the subject. The excavations at the "shore" temple Mâmallâpuram, which I conducted in 1884, revealed a plan very similar. Some have supposed that the Kailâsanâdha temple must, originally, have been a Jain shrine. The popular idea is, that such was the case; but this, like some other popular myths, will be found, on examination, to be a fallacy. In the great wealth of sculpture represented, there is not a single figure that could by any stretch of the imagination, be called Jain; and in a building such as this—where almost every available space is sculptured with mythological scenes—this is of itself, almost a convincing proof. If the temple had been once a Jain shrine, we would surely have found some such figures on it, but not a single one is so. The feature that has evidently led to this error, is the peculiarity of the groups of cells ranged along each side of the courtyard; and this, though a novel arrangement as far as temples in this part of the Peninsula are concerned, is still seen in a modified form in many or most of the large Saivite temples in these districts. The cells were originally occupied by *liṅgas*, each with its separate name, and representing a different manifestation of Śiva. Several of these still remain in position. The usual *somasutra* opening,—for carrying off the surplus water used in the *pûja*—is seen through the side walls opposite each cell; they could not therefore, have been cells for devotees. Moreover, the Pallava Grantha inscriptions on the face of each, give the names, either of the different *liṅgas* or titles of the king who executed the buildings. They are all Śaivite appellations. Granting that these inscriptions (on the cells) might have been executed afterwards,—although there are no grounds for believing they have been—the very sculptures themselves, on each, leave no doubt as to the purpose for which they were intended, or the religion to which they were devoted. In other temples, the *liṅgas* of this sort, are arranged in a row, on a platform along the *prâkâra*, placed side by side, but without a separate cell for each *liṅga*. The arrangement employed at the Kailâsanâdha, is probably a northern idea brought south, after some of their expeditions in that quarter; and moreover, as it has been supposed that their sculpture was also executed by workers from the north, this assumption may perhaps prove correct. An arrangement, somewhat resembling the cells, is seen at the Kailâsa rock temple at Elûra.[24] It is, however, evidently a later development of the cells proper, being probably a transition between these, and the usual verandah round the interior of the court, seen in more modern temples. The idea of a group of minor shrines around the principal one, is also seen in the example quoted, but differing in their plan from that at the Kâñchîpuram temple.

---

[24] Fergusson: *Ind. and Eas. Arch.*, p. 334, *pl.* 186.

As the same typical style is found in all these Pallava temples,—with repetitions, or modifications of the same features occurring in each,—a detailed description of the notable points in the principal example may be sufficient for all purposes; with a general outline of the characteristics of design, and modifications or advancements of the style found in the lesser examples.

Most of the temples under note, have evidently always been devoted to the worship of Śiva; the sculptures are generally representations of scenes from the Śaivite mythology, and the inscriptions seem to bear this out.

GENERAL PLAN.

(Plate No. XXIV.)

The plan is comprised in a large, and a smaller courtyard, with a central group of shrines placed towards the western extremity of the large one. The central shrine is surmounted by a lofty pyramidal tower. Originally, this group of shrines has stood completely detached. The entrance to the central *vimâna* has been from the east, and still is, although now through the modern *ardhamaṇḍapam*.

At each corner, and on the north, south and west sides is a smaller shrine. The original door to the *vimâna*, on the east side, was through a porch with a projection similar to these exterior lesser shrines. It is now blocked up by the *ardhamaṇḍapam*. Each of these shrines, and the porch, has a smaller tower, which rises up to, and is grouped alongside the greater one. Near the base at each corner and face, between the projecting shrines, a large *nandi* is placed on the ground.

On each side of the large court, is ranged a continuous series of cells, each with a small tower and *śikhara* over it. These *śikharas* have originally stood with their summits appearing above the wall head of the court, with *nandis* and elephants placed alternately on the wall head between them. This would form a most effective grouping as a whole, from the outside; but, for purposes of defence, or for some caprice or other, the spaces between these *śikharas* have been blocked up with masonry, composed of stone, brickwork and mud, so that now the outside of this court, forms a continuous line of dead wall. The superincumbent weight of this additional masonry, not originally contemplated, has caused large gaps or cracks in several parts of the walls on which it is placed, notably a few on the south side. The cell towers still show on the inside, but not on the outer face of the courtyard wall.* On the north and south sides of this court, the cells directly opposite the central *vimâna* are larger than the others, and have a higher tower over them. The centre of the western wall has an entrance *gôpuram*, with a similar tower over; the door is however, now blocked up. In front of the large central shrine—to the east—is the *mahâmaṇḍapam* which has once stood detached from the central group of shrines; but to suit modern requirements, is now joined to the shrine by the *ardhamaṇḍapam*. The entrance door to this latter building, is up a flight of steps, through a verandah on the south side; a perforated stone window opens into the *mahâmaṇḍapam*. This latter structure is open on the four sides, with return walls at each of the corners of the building. The north and south sides have simple

* See footnote on page 16.

openings, with a pilaster on each jamb of the door, while the east and west sides, are divided each by two massive piers. The space inside is divided into compartments by similar supports placed at very short intervals.

To the east of the large court, is a lesser one; and to enter the temple, it must first be passed through. A lesser temple stands in a line with the centre of the wall dividing the two courts, so that a half of it projects into each. A door is then formed in the wall on each side of this temple, by either of which, the large court is entered through the lesser. The smaller court has an exterior door on its east, north and south sides. Ranged along its eastern face are a series of eight small shrines, each with a tower over it. They are open towards the east, and are similar in design to some of the *rathas* at Mâmallâpuram. The shrines immediately adjacent to the lesser court, or those immediately on each side of its eastern entrance, are connected by the wall of the court; the others stand in a line north and south, and have once been completely detached from each other, though now the space between them has been filled in with rough rubble work, blocking up the sculptured panels on their sides.

About 60 yards east of these, a large stone *nandi* stands on a platform; and between it, and the *rathas*, is a circular well—5 feet in diameter—with some sculptured *râkshasas* cut on its walls some distance below the surface of the ground. North of the *nandi* is a square reservoir or tank, with stone steps on each of the four sides. The temple has seemingly been originally comprised in the larger court only, and the lesser afterwards added; the space of time between the two however, could only have been a very few years, if even that, for the style of the two is identical, and the addition of the lesser seems as though it had been an afterthought of the builders of the large court.

That it was an addition is evident, as there are pilasters, with *yâlis* and riders, which return along the outside of the eastern wall of the large court at regular intervals, and some are thus in the interior of the lesser one. From their spacing, it is clearly seen that the north and south walls of the east enclosure abut against the *yâlis*, in a way that would not have occurred had the lesser court been part of the original design. This eastern wall of the large court also bears evidence of having been partly demolished in the centre, to admit of the placing of the temple which stands immediately between the two enclosures. This temple must therefore have been a later addition.

The plan bears a similarity in many respects to that of the "shore" temple at Mâmallâpuram, as shewn by the excavations previously referred to. In that temple, the shrines stand with a detached *maṇḍapam* in front; and on each of the sides of the court was found a raised platform with pier bases remaining, as if cells, similar to those at the Kailâsanâdha temple had been placed on them. The *nandis* placed on the ground at each corner and face of the large shrine, were also found. The two plans of course differ in some points, even as other buildings—though in one style of architecture,—may vary in their arrangement, according to the caprices of their several designers. But a close examination reveals the fact that the same general idea prevails in, and has been in the minds of the architects of both.

DETAILS OF ARCHITECTURE AND SCULPTURE.

In the sculptures we find—as before remarked—a complete representation of the Śaivite mythology. Śiva shewn as the great creator and destroyer, with the deities Brahmâ and Vishṇu each severally represented doing homage to him.

The wealth of design, superiority and minuteness of execution so largely shown, are simply marvellous. Whether the designs were suggested by some master hand, or left to the individual sculptors themselves, is somewhat difficult to know, but the continuity of arrangement, and grouping of the entire series, show a thorough mastery of every detail of the art. Most of the carvings are covered with plaster, and this to a certain extent hides their beauties, but in the many places where it has fallen off, the original work is clearly seen. The plastering must have been done at some late period, for the stonework underneath, has a weatherworn appearance, only traceable to the action of many centuries of time. The stone floral work is most minutely cut, and, in places where the plaster has been laid on, over the stone carvings, the work underneath has been roughly represented by outline impressions made by some implement on the wet mortar, resembling the work which it covers. The plaster has done one good thing, in preserving the stonework from the effects of the weather; for, being in a soft friable material, the carvings would, in most cases, if not thus protected, have been almost entirely worn away.

This is seen in the Tripurântakêśvara and Airâvatêśvara temples, where plastering has not been resorted to, till the stone has been considerably corroded; and in plastering over, the weatherworn hollows have had to be filled up with brickwork before the stucco could be laid on.

Comparing the weatherworn appearance of these buildings with other temples in the same district, of Chôḷa date,—and evidently of the eleventh century,—the difference between them is too marked to be the result of even a few centuries only; and considering that the stone at the Kailâsanâdha temple has been covered with plaster—at what date it is difficult to say, but probably several centuries at the least—while the later examples which I quote, have not been so protected, it only supports the architectural evidence of the early foundation of this temple.

DESCRIPTION.

The *nandi maṇḍapam* to the east of the temple has only a basement remaining, on which stand four *yâḷi* piers—one at each corner—and a large *nandi* in the centre. It originally has had,—or been intended to have had—a roof, but no traces of it now remain. It would probably be similar to, though larger than those at the Tripurântakêśvara and Muktêśvara temples, (see Plates Nos. CXIII and Fig. 4 in LXIX). The lowest, or sub-base is of freestone, with two granite plinths over; then a broad freestone course carved with *gandharvas*; while above that, is a semi-octagonal base moulding with leaf ornaments on the angles and fronts. This ornament is a square, and a somewhat lozenge shaped quatrefoil leaf placed alternately, and running along the faces of the moulding; lotus leaves are on the bevelled sides: the same design is found on the *vimâna* tower, and other bases.[95]

[95] A somewhat similar ornament is common in Châlukyan work, but applied differently. In examples of that style, it is never applied to basements, but is generally seen on the jamb mouldings of doors. Its form is slightly different; but the design is practically the same. In Pallava works, on the contrary, it is only found on the bases of buildings.

6

Above the semi-octagon, is a square top moulding, with sunk panels, and small projecting *yâḷis* placed at intervals on its face.

The four *yâḷi* piers stand on the top of the last member, one at each corner. The large *nandi* is placed in the centre, with its head in the usual position facing the temple to the west. Its height is about 6 feet, and length 7 feet. It is built in courses of freestone, and has been profusely decorated with representations of jewel ornaments: the traces of these remain, much weatherworn.

RATHAS.

(SEE PLATE NO. XXV.)

On the east elevation of the temple, as before stated, eight small shrines stand in a row from north to south on each side of the eastern entrance, six on the right, and two on the left. It would seem from the placing of these, that it had been intended to have an equal number on each side—*i.e.*, six on the left, to correspond with the number on the right. The last *ratha* [96] on the left—or that on the extreme south—is incomplete in its carving, and it would seem that the intention had been to complete each before commencing another. Or probably, those which might have stood in a line to the left of it have been demolished to make way for the road, which runs along the south of the temple.

The *ratha* on the extreme left, stands completely detached. It is a square shrine, with carved panels on the back of the chamber; these are, two figures (Śiva and Pârvati) in a sitting posture, and some others under. They are much decayed, and the design can, with difficulty be made out; it seems to represent the same group that we find in the others, *i.e.*, Śiva seated with Pârvati on his left, and umbrellas over, held by attendants on each side. This grouping and design are seen in many of the large courtyard cells and shrines. It is identical with those on the shrine walls of the Mâmallâpuram caves. On the exterior wall is a *yâḷi* at each of the four corners. They are only partly carved, some of the rough blocks having been scarcely touched by the chisel: each *yâḷi* block supports a pilaster, and these have moulded caps over. On the back and sides are the rough blocks of what were intended to be sculptured panels similar to the others. Between these panel spaces and the corner *yâḷis*, are small pilasters.

A small platform is in front, with *yâḷi* piers (blocks uncarved), each having its capital complete.

The basement is a square granite plinth, and square freestone course with semi-octagonal moulding over; the upper base is a square granite course on which the superstructure rests. On the wall-head—over the pilasters—are brackets which carry the cornice; all these are much weatherworn. Traces of carved floral ornaments remain on the cornice. Above, is a series of small mouldings with carved projections at intervals; each moulding is recessed or stepped back a short space from that immediately below it. Over these, is an upright portion of wall with carved figures in the centre of each space. On each side of the figures are small pilasters, with seated *yâḷis* at the corners. A double cornice caps this, and the whole is surmounted by an octagonal domed *śikhara* with carved pedimental ornaments on

---

[96] As these shrines are very similar to the monoliths at Mâmallâpuram, known by the name of "*rathás*" the term is here used advisedly.

each side. In the centre of the most of these cornices are a series of vertical holes about four inches in diameter. It would seem as if these had been intended for the poles of banners placed there during festivals.

The *ratha* on the right of the last, is practically the same, but is in a more complete condition. The *yâḷis* on the piers are carved. Inside the shrine is a black stone *liṅga*. *Dvârapâlas* are carved on each side of the door. This shrine is attached, at its north-west corner, to the east and south walls of the eastern court.

The panels on the exterior of the walls are carved. That on the south side has a seated figure of Śiva with long matted hair; he sits under a tree, with a *nâga* on his left: some symbols in his right hand are too weatherworn to be clearly distinguished.

Between the panel and the corner pilasters, are traces of carvings, but almost obliterated by the action of the weather. On the north and west walls, there are also sculptures, but the east and south walls of the court abut against them.

To the right of this shrine—on the southern portion of the abutting eastern court wall,—are pilasters placed at intervals, with a basement under, and a double cornice over.

The doorway to the east court has *yâḷis* at the corners, pilasters on the angles of the door and a cornice over. Above the cornice is an upright portion of wall rising above the court walls on either side. In the centre of this, is a panel with Śiva, Pârvati and attendants: Brahmâ and Vishṇu are shewn worshipping them. At the angles of this portion, and over the cornice last mentioned, *nandis* are placed. The whole doorway is then crowned by a barrel-shaped pediment, lying parallel with the wall through which the door enters. On this, are a series of leaf carvings overlaid with plaster.

To the right of the doorway is the northern portion of the east wall of the lesser court. Like the wall on the left of the central entrance it has a basement, pilasters at intervals, and a double cornice over.

To the right of this wall, which abuts against it, is the third *ratha*, numbering them successively from the left. The design of this, and in fact the whole group of eight, are much the same as those already detailed, the only differences being in the sculptures and their relative states of preservation from decay. The base mouldings of this (third) shrine are much weatherworn. On the granite portion is an inscription in Pallava Granḍha characters. The *yâḷis* on the front pillars have tusks, and twisted trunks. A *liṅga* stands in the shrine, and there is a panel, with Śiva and Pârvati, carved on the back of the chamber. The *dvârapâlas* of the door are much decayed.

The fourth *ratha* from the left, has a *liṅga* in the shrine. The basement is much decayed, as also the shrine panel, and most of the carvings and mouldings. The *yâlis* in front differ from those on the *ratha* previously mentioned in that they have no tusks. The *rathas* from third to eighth, are connected by walls of modern masonry.

The fifth is generally the same as the previous one. On the semi-octagonal base is an inscription somewhat illegible; another is on the granite sur-base. On the front and sides of the projecting façade are small elephants.

The sixth has the basement very much hollowed out. One of the *yâḷi* pillars has been removed and a plain stone substituted. A *liṅga* is inside, with a panel on the back of the shrine. The door *dvârapâlas* are much worn away. Under the sub-base, a granite course of the foundations is seen above ground. This course continues right along under the following *rathas* without any break between them, forming a continuous platform on which the superstructures rest.

It no doubt also extends in the opposite direction to the extreme left; but, in the case of those *rathas* previously mentioned, it is under the soil.

The seventh is the same as the others, except that the door *dvârapâlas* have elephant trunks. There are two inscriptions, one on the granite base, and the other on the semi-octagonal moulding.

The eighth, and last *ratha*—continuing the numbering from the left—has the lower base mouldings much worn; a portion of the granite sur-course is also away. The carvings on the *dvârapâlas* are very distinctly shewn; in their ears are jewel holes.[27] The left *yâli* pillar is away. The right pillar has no figure carved on it, and the present stone support evidently replaces the original pier which has been removed. On the north side of this *ratha* is a panel with a standing figure of Śiva with matted hair; he has two hands; a serpent is over his shoulder; and a worshipper stands on each side, with uplifted hands joined lotus shape. Over the panelled niche in which the figures stand, is a floral pedimental ornament, only partly carved. The central portion shews representations of two *yâlis*, with drooping floral ornament on each side. This is very commonly shewn on most of the niches in the temple; and a similar design is seen at the Vaikuṇṭha Perumâḷ temple;[28] the cave temple at Śiyamangalam; and, at some of the *rathas* and cave temples at Mâmallâpuram. It is a feature, striking in its individuality, and shews the close connection between the architectural period of the groups.

In the succeeding Chôḷa, and later Dravidian temples, the same feature is common enough, but it has a distinctly different character. Like other details in successive developments of the primary style, the modifications of various members are each characteristic of the several successive periods of Dravidian architecture. The difference in each becomes more striking as the style advances.

The spaces between these *rathas* being—as I have mentioned—filled up, it is impossible to see what sculptures are on their sides; these,—unless they have been damaged when the spaces were filled in—should be in a much better state of preservation than most of the other panels, which are exposed to, and have suffered severely from the weather.

Returning along the back of the *rathas* from the eighth,—or that on the extreme north—and proceeding south, I shall note the sculptures on each in succession.

The group on the back of the eighth—retaining the numbering already given—has Śiva on an elephant; the death noose is in his left hand; his right foot is uplifted on the elephant's head; he holds in the lower right hand a trident, and in the lower left a *nâga*. He is represented as stripping the elephant's skin, which he waves aloft in his two upper hands. At his sides are a standing figure of a devotee on the left, and two *gandharvas* on the right.

The panelled back of the seventh *ratha* is similar to that just described, but in this case Śiva has six hands. Under, are some *gandharva* figures. The small panel on the right has a gracefully posed female figure; that on the left a male. These are clearly cut in stone, without traces of plaster remaining. The ornament over the niche is covered with plaster.

The back of the sixth *ratha* has a figure seated on a chariot. The vehicle is being drawn by two horses; the front is shewn, and between them is a carved and moulded shaft. In Siva's two left hands are a *nâga* and trident; one of his right is held in the boon-conferring

[27] N.B.—See page 8.

[28] See Plate No. LXVII.

attitude (*abhayahasta*); the other hands hold various symbols. In each panel on the sides of the central one is a minor celestial being, each with four hands. Under the granite surbase are small elephant blocks.

On the back of the fifth *ratha* is a seated Śaivite figure in the central panel. It has eight hands and the usual Śaiva symbols in each. The lower portion is much weatherworn. In the panel on the right of the central one is a female figure in a strikingly graceful attitude. The figure in the left panel is too much decayed to be clearly distinguished. The ornament over, is partly covered with plaster. An inscription is on the base.

The sculptures on the back of the fourth *ratha* are much decayed; some of the symbols only—such as the axe and noose, held by the principal figure—can be made out.

EXTERIOR OF THE COURT.

On the north exterior side of the large courtyard are twenty-two pilasters at regular intervals, and one at each of the north-east and north-west corners. Each pilaster has a *yâḷi*, with rider seated on reverse sides at each alternate bay. A granite course runs along the lower basement of the wall. Between the *yâḷis* are the openings for carrying off the water from the cells on the interior of the wall.

On the west exterior side,—in the centre—is a gateway with a small *gôpuram* tower over; the door is now blocked up. An elephant and *gandharva* are seated on the wall head, and an upper central panel has Śiva seated in *yôgâsana* with his hands across his knees. On this façade of the court wall there are five *yâḷi* pilasters on either side of the central doorway. A continuous cornice runs along the top of the ancient wall; above this is the modern portion, blocking up the cell *śikharas* before alluded to.

The south exterior side of the great courtyard is spaced by pilasters, similar to those on the northern side. Numbering from the south-west corner there are large cracks in the wall between the first and second, fourth and fifth, and eighteenth and nineteenth pilasters. These fissures are seemingly caused by the great weight of the modern superstructure built on the top of the ancient wall; a mass of material, which the original foundations were never intended to carry. It would be well, if the temple authorities could be induced to remove it, as it would conduce both to the stability of the court walls and add to the external beauty of the structure in general. Should the cracks, referred to, bring down portions of the wall,—and in time they certainly will,—the openings so made, if repaired at all, would most assuredly be filled up with unsightly brick and plaster work. Should this superstructure be removed, the *śikharas*, elephants and *nandis* would be exposed to view, and the temple better seen in every way.*

INTERIOR OF THE SMALL (EAST) COURT.

On the interior side of the east wall, on each side of the central entrance, are pilasters with figures between, three panels on each side. The panels immediately on each side of the door have *dvârapâlas*: the others, figures of Śiva seated with his attendants: these are

* As before marked this has been done.

all covered with stucco. Projecting into the two east corners of this court are the *rathas* (Nos. 2 & 3). In the north-east corner is a stone with a well-carved figure of Śiva seated on a bull. In Śiva's two right hands are a trident and *nâga*; the left hands also hold other symbols. On the panels of the *ratha* projecting into the south-east corner, are figures of Śiva seated in *yôgâsana*. On a stone of the base, on the south inner side of the east entrance, is a short inscription in foliated characters. On each of the north and south sides of this court is a doorway, at present blocked up with mud. A panel on the left side of the south door has a seated *yôgi* with a *kuja* in his left hand; two minor figures are under.

Next to the last panel is a sculpture representing Pârvatî and the lion. She has a trident and umbrella; the figures are covered with plaster, but the design, though smaller, seems similar in its grouping to another of the same subject close by. This other will be described in its proper place.

On the right of the last is a small shrine, having the back panel sculptured with seated figures of Śiva and Pârvatî. Śiva has been *converted* into Brahmâ, by the addition—in plaster only—of a face on either side of his original one. Attendants stand at the sides of the central group. There have been two *yâli* piers in front, but these are now away, and in their places are two brick piers.

The panel to the right is a large one, and has a sculptured group of twelve sages, who seem to be listening to the exhortations of the philosophic Śiva (*Dakshinâmûrti*), who is represented seated under a banyan tree in a panel opposite this one, on the south side wall of the central shrine in this court. The panel with the sages occupies a position on the south wall of the court, and the two panels exactly face each other. This ingenious arrangement is adopted on the opposite side of this court, and also on the north and south sides of the large *vimâna*.

On the north side of this (lesser) court, at the north-east corner, is the figure of Śiva and the bull already described. At the same corner is the *ratha* (No. 3) corresponding to that on the opposite side of the east entrance above noted. The panel on this one is however, different from the other. In this, a figure of Lakshmî is seated on a lotus; she holds two lotus buds in her hands; a zone is round her waist; a garland on her neck; and a crown on her head: elephants pour water over her.

In the north wall of the same court is a built-up doorway, opposite that in the south wall. On the left of this door is a figure of Ganapati, with umbrella and two *chauries* over; in his left hands are symbols—one a lotus, but the other undistinguishable. In the right are a noose, and another which seems an elephant goad. The walls over the north and south doors to this enclosure are somewhat ruined.

On the same wall as the last panel, and to the left, is a small shrine attached to the wall; it stands opposite the one on the south side; and the two are similar, with the exception that the *yâli* piers of this one are complete. To the left of the shrine is a large panel; it is opposite the large one noted on the south side. The subject is much the same in both cases; in this panel, eleven seated sages are listening to the exhortations of Śiva, who is represented in a panel on the north side of the central shrine. He is armed with different symbolical weapons, and seems to be preaching war.

MAHÊNDRAVARMÊŚVARA SHRINE.

The small temple which stands in the centre of the wall dividing the lesser and large courts bears the modern name of Nârada liṅga temple. From an inscription however, on the side of the stair, the ancient name seems to have been Mahêndravarmêśvaragṛiham. The wall which divides the two courts abuts against the north and south walls of this shrine, so that a portion of it projects into each court; the entrance is from the east.

The lower base has two courses of granite; above these, is a freestone course, with a row of sculptured *gandharvas*. These figures are represented with their hands raised above their heads with the palms of their hands flattened against the moulding over, as if they were intended to be shown as supporting the building.[99]

Over the figures is a semi-octagonal member, carved on each of the bevelled surfaces with leaf ornaments. The sur-base is recessed back from the last, and has blocks carved into elephants' heads, under each pilaster on the façades of the superstructure: the basement is finished with an inscribed granite course. The door enters on the east side; the granite block on each side of the stair leading up to the entrance is carved into a sort of scroll (see Plates Nos. XXVI and XXVII), with the name Mahêndravarmêśvaragṛiham on the outer sides in Pallava Grantha characters. The plan is a simple porch or *adytum*, off which the shrine enters. The sides of the *adytum* are sculptured with figures considerably over life size; the back walls of the porch and shrine have also carved figure subjects.

In the interior of the porch on the right side, is a row of the *hamsa* or sacred geese; over these, is a large kneeling figure with eight hands; the symbols on the right side, are, a *chaurie*, noose, and others broken and covered with plaster: in two of the left hands are two balls, probably representing lime fruits.

The panel opposite the last, on the left inner side of the porch, has a large finely carved figure of Jîmûtakêtu or the cloud bannered (Śiva). He is represented with matted hair; the right knee bent; he has a richly carved crown, and neck, arm and leg ornaments. Over his left shoulder is a garland, with rings, of what seem intended for bones; another has alternate square and round ornaments, on each of which is a sculptured skull: these reach down to his ankles. The waist ornament is broad, and has several bands of different ornamental designs. The anklets are in circles of balls; and on the feet are well carved and ornamented sandals, (*pâdaraksha*). On each sandal, the *kamiḻ*—or small knob between the toes—is shown. On his left side is the three-hooded *nâga*, with its tail twisted upwards, and resting on his hand. The cloud banner is held in a left hand over the shoulder, goes behind him and droops over the right, down to the waist: on the upper portion of the same side is—apparently— a club. A worshipping female figure stands on his right; two females are on the left, one of which, profusely ornamented with jewels, is kneeling and worshipping: the other female on the left side supports one of Śiva's left hands. There are some other minor attendants in the group.

This panel is remarkably striking in the arrangement and execution of the whole design, even the smallest ornaments being clearly and beautifully cut.

On the back wall of the porch is the door to the shrine; on either side of it is a niche, each with a figure of Lakshmî: between the niches and door, are *dvârapâlas* with *chauries*.

---

[99] See remarks on page 19.

In the shrine, is a large black stone moulded *liṅga.* On the back wall, in a niche, is a panel, sculptured with seated figures of Śiva and Pârvati, with Brahmâ, Vishṇu, and attendants worshipping.

EXTERIOR OF MAHÊNDRAVARMÊŚVARA GṚIHAM.

On the south side of this shrine—facing into the lesser court—is the large panel before referred to, as being opposite the sculptured group of twelve sages (p. 26). It represents the figure of Dakshiṇâmûrti, or Śiva in his *yôgi* seat, under a banyan tree. He has four hands; in the upper right is a noose; and in one of the left is a serpent; his hair is matted; and his knees are bound together with a cloth. In the same panel are a male, and female and two deer.

Over the niche is a central figure of Gaṇapati, with a *yâḷi* on each side, from whose jaws, carved foliage spreads along either side of the top, and droops down, forming a canopy over the principal figures of the panel below. On each side of the large panel is a set of three small ones; in the right lower are two figures seated cross legged; they have matted hair, and are seemingly *yôgis*; the panel over has a lion and two *gandharvas*; the top panel has a musician playing to amuse Śiva.

The lowest of the three panels—on the left of the central one—has two figures, one of which is a *yôgi* with beard, matted hair and crown: the upper tier of panels is similar to the right side.

The features of all these figures have rather a marked form of countenance; the noses are pointed and flat, and give a curious expression to the face. They are similar in this respect to the figures on the bases of the piers at the Kachchêśvara temple, and probably represent the type common among some of the tribes in early times in the country, (see Plates Nos. XXVI, XXI and XX).

On the east exterior face of this shrine, the central feature is the door, with a large *dvârapâla* on each side. At each of the north-east and south-east exterior corners of the building is a large *yâḷi.*

The north side has a design similar in its main features and grouping, to the south side. The principal figure is Śiva, but, in this case, he is shown in a fierce attitude, armed with numerous symbolical weapons, and seemingly preaching war to his disciples seated in the panel directly opposite, (see page 26). He has eight hands, the upper right and left support an elephant's skin over his head; in the right, are drum, club and trident; one of the left touches his crown; another has a noose, and the lowest is empty. Over the figure is a row of *gandharvas*, and a cornice with carved blocks.

EAST DOORS TO THE INNER COURT.

Mention has already been made of the east wall of the larger court which abuts against the north and south walls of the temple just described. Through this wall—one on either side of this shrine,—is a door, entering from the small into the greater court.

The door on the south side has, on its right jamb, a few remaining letters of an ancient inscription. The left jamb has a boldly carved representation of Pârvati and the lion. She has sixteen hands; over her right are an umbrella and two balls; the right hands have noose, shield, and drum; two hands bend her bow, which is large and extends right across her body from top to bottom of the panel. On the same side is a three-hooded *nâga*. On the left side are a trident, a portion of the bow, war club, and conch; one hand is under the umbrella, and the remaining hands on this side are unarmed. The lion is shown with much vigour of expression; the tusks and claws are all clearly cut, and the neck and body of the animal are decorated with minutely carved jewels.

This panel is free of plaster, and the striking attitude of the figures, arrangement and grouping of the different members, and the artistic finish of the workmanship can be distinctly seen. The design, grouping and general effect of this panel are exactly similar to the well-known sculpture at Mâmallâpuram, representing Pârvati on the lion, fighting the bull-headed Mahishâsura. In the Kâñchîpuram sculpture, the latter figure is omitted, but it is otherwise almost identical with the left half of the one at the Seven Pagodas. (See Plate No. XXIX.)

The east door entering the large court on the north side of the Mahêndravarma shrine, has the remains of a long inscription on the left side. On the other is a panel, similar in style and execution to that just described; the subject is however different. The other showed Pârvati, this represents Lakshmî seated on a lotus, with her feet resting on another of the same flowers; she has also a lotus bud in each hand. On each side stands a female attendant with *chaurie*. Over Lakshmi's head are, what seem to be the five hoods of a snake; and an elephant with water pot is on either side. There are traces of colour on this panel. (Plate No. XXX.)

INNER COURT.

Entering the large court, the first sculptures are those on the back of the Mahêṇḍravarma shrine.

The base moulding round the back of this shrine is the same as that on the sides already described (p. 27); the upper member of the basement on this side is also inscribed.

The central back panel is a large one; the principal figures are Śiva and Pârvati seated on a throne, with three *chaurie*-bearing attendants. On each side is a *yâḷi*, and niches, with figures of Vishṇu, Lakshmî, and *gandharvas*; under the panels are two large elephants' heads represented as supporting the groups. At each of the corners of the building are *yâḷis* with riders and *gandharvas*. Over these sculptures is an elaborate cornice; the lower member is sculptured with a row of supporting *gandharvas*; a pedimented and double cornice over; and above the last, on the first storey of the tower is a set of three panelled sculptures. The central panel has Śiva as a *yôgi*, with an attendant on right and left, and two detached *yâḷis* in front. The panel on either side has each a many-armed figure. The upper portion of the tower is formed of three sets of cornices, the top tier having a central figure of Narasimha; the figure is covered with comparatively modern plaster work, so it is difficult to distinguish what it may have been originally. The whole tower is crowned by a barrel-shaped *śikhara* with leaf ornaments and finials (See Plate No. XXXI).

CELL SCULPTURES.

In proceeding with the sculptures on the series of cells on the four side of the large court, it will be convenient to begin with those immediately to the south of the Mahêṇḍravarma shrine on the east side of the court, and continue the numbering in succession, round the south, west, north and north half of the east sides, returning to the starting point.

All these cells have originally had their *śikharas* appearing over the old wall-head of the enclosing wall, with *nandis*, and elephants alternately, between each. Some of the *śikharas* are now ruined, and their place has been plastered over; this is notably the case on the east wall, which is thicker than the other three, so that when the modern work was added to the wall head, and carried up—with the same thickness as the ancient substructure—to overtop the small towers, it almost completely covered them. The animals placed between the cell towers, only appear out of the thickness of the recent masonry, at intervals.

All the cells have had inscriptions on three members of the basements, though some have now been worn away; the lowest is—in all cases—foliated.

No. 1 cell.—Immediately to the south of the Mahêṇḍravarma shrine, is open in front, and has panelled seated figures of Śiva, Pârvati, and child.

Space between Nos. 1 and 2.—Śiva and Pârvati.

No. 2.—Open in front; same as No. 1.

Space between Nos. 2 and 3, same as No. 1.

No. 3.—Same.

Space between No. 3 and south-east corner recess, same.

The recess in the south-east corner is not a shrine proper like the others, so it may be omitted in the numbering; it is open towards the west and has a bas-relief of Gaṇapati.

Returning along the south wall, the space between the south-east corner recess and No. 4 cell, has Pârvati seated under a banyan tree; one large and two small elephants are on the left side. A *yôgi* sits, with his knees bound, on the back of the large animal. A female attendant is on the right.

No. 4 is open towards the east, as also are the others on this wall; the sculptures are on the outer front of the screen walls enclosing them from the *prâkâra* of the court. This cell has Pârvati and the lion, with symbols, and a general design similar to that already described on the left door between the two courts (see p. 28). In this panel, an additional *gandharva* figure stands on the left. The upper portion of the sculpture is plastered over, but the lower part has the stone exposed, and shows its delicate cutting. (See Plate No. XXXII, Fig. 1.)

The space between Nos. 4 and 5, has the usual panel of Śiva and Pârvati.

No. 5, opens towards the east; it has a seated Śaivite figure, with four hands and symbols; these latter are undistinguishable through a covering of plaster. (Plate No. XXXII, Fig. 2.)

Between Nos. 5 and 6.—Śiva and Pârvati. No. 6, Pârvati under a tree, with a female *chaurie* bearer on each upper side of the panel; two figures and a kneeling worshipper are on each lower side. (Plate No. XXXIII, Fig 5.)

Between Nos. 6 and 7.—Śiva and Pârvati.

No. 7.—A large Śaivite figure with four hands, on a chariot drawn by two horses; over the horses' heads is a pillar supporting a bull. Over the bull is one, and on the extreme right of the figure are two *gandharvas*. On the left of the charioteer, and in front of the vehicle, is a Brahmâ. (Plate No. XXXIII, Fig. 6.)

Between Nos. 7 and 8.—Pârvati seated under a tree; a deer is on her left, and two are underneath; a bird, probably a peacock, is on a branch of the tree; a female attendant is on her right.

No. 8.—Śiva riding on a *bhûta;* four figures with various symbols are on the left. (Plate No. XXXIII, Fig. 1.)

Between Nos. 8 and 9.—Śiva and Pârvati.

No. 9.—Is rather a curious group; the principal figure is Narasiṁha; he is supported by a figure on the right, and they fight with another one on the left; a pedestal stands in the centre. (Plate No. XXXIII, Fig. 2.)

Between Nos. 9 and 10.—Pârvati under a tree; a female attendant is on her right and a *yôgi* on her left; beneath the last are three bulls with long curved horns.

No. 10.—Has a number of figures with arrangement and attitudes very spirited and well designed. Two chief figures occupy the centre of the panel; one is Brahmâ on the right, supported by six-armed *gandharvas* who spring from a lotus flower with leaves and buds under: a worshipping figure kneels beneath the lotus. Another on Brahmâ's right is being pushed towards him by a figure—probably Yama the god of death. Two others occupy positions near Yama, evidently waiting their turn. (Plate No. CXXIII, Fig. 6.)

Between Nos. 10 and 11.—Pârvati under a tree, attendant, bird and two elephants.

No. 11.—Is a many-armed Vaishnava figure, with conch, club, bow, sword and shield. His left foot is stretched up, measuring the hanging head of a snake; two figures are on his left. On the left of the panel is Vishṇu in his dwarf incarnation (*Vâmana*), with the king and queen. A *Jâmbavantu* is in the upper portion of the panel. (Plate No. CXXIII, Fig. 7.)

Between Nos. 11 and 12.—Śiva and Pârvati. This panel shows the churning of the ocean. The five-hooded serpent is coiled round the base of the mountain (Mandâra). Vishṇu, on the left, holds the mountain; and the *Dêvas* on the right, who are represented by five figures, twist the tail of the serpent. At Vishṇu's left hand, and between him and the hill, stands a *Dêva*, on whom Vishṇu places one of his hands. Four *gandharvas* are on the mountain. A horse, probably Indra's, (Uchchaiśravas), which has just sprung from the ocean, is on the extreme left. (Plate No. XXXIII, Fig. 3.)

Between Nos. 12 and 13.—Pârvati and attendants, birds, and two elephants.

No. 13.—A central figure of Śiva with five *gandharvas* worshipping under. A male, holding a symbol, stands on his left, with a *gandharvas* over. Above these, is a five-hooded *nâga*, as also another on Śiva's right. (Plate No. XXXIII, Fig. 4.)

Between Nos. 13 and 14.—Same as between Nos. 12 and 13

No. 14.—Shows Śiva cutting off one of the heads of Brahmâ, and holding it in one of his left hands; Brahmâ sits in a dejected attitude on the left. A devotee—with arms crossed in amazement—sits under Śiva on Brahmâ's right. In Śiva's right hands are sword, trident, snake and noose; in his left are Brahmâ's head, and broken symbols. There is not much plaster on the panel, and the deep and bold cutting is seen to advantage, giving fine effects of light and shade. (Plate No. XXXIV, Fig. 1.)

Between Nos. 14 and 15.—Śiva and Pârvati.

No. 15.—Shows Śiva—as a hunter—fighting with, and slaying the king, who was afterwards turned into a pig. Two figures are shown with right and left legs advanced. An animal on the under right side of the panel seems to represent Varâha. (Plate No. XXXIV, Fig. 2.)

Between Nos. 15 and 16.—Pârvati with an attendant on her left; two elephants, and a bird on her right.

No. 16.—Śiva in *yôgâsana*, resting on the shoulders of a devotee. Two *yôgis* sit in meditation, on what seem to be clouds. (Plate No. XXXV, Fig. 1.)

Between Nos. 16 and 17.—Śiva and Pârvati.

No. 17.—Śiva with club, bow, trident and noose, stands on a platform supported by a devotee, and the five-hooded human-faced Âdisêsha. Vishṇu on an attendant, worships Śiva; two hands are closed in adoration; other two hold his emblems, the conch and discus. (Plate No. XXXV, Fig. 2.)

Between Nos. 17 and 18.—Śiva—armed with a large club—and his wife Pârvati.

No. 18.—Śiva kills a double-headed *râkshasa* with his trident. A figure sits under the weapon; three others, and a snake are on his left; the head of another appears on the right. A figure on Śiva's left—midway up the panel—has a tiger's legs, and probably represents Vyâghrapâda. On the upper right portion of the panel, Śiva is seen seated with his wife Pârvati, soaring through the sky. (Plate No. XXXVI, Fig. 1.)

Between Nos. 18 and 19.—Pârvati stands, with two figures on each side. On the west side of this space are two representations of Brahmâ—one kneeling, and the other standing; over are two *gandharvas*.

No. 19.—Is a large cell, open in front. It has a *yâḷi dvârapâla* on each corner; and two *yâḷi* pillars on the platform in front. On the back of the cell, Brahmâ sits with a figure on each side; and two *gandharvas* over, worshipping. (Plate No. XXXVI, Fig. 2.)

A tower of different outline, and higher than the others, surmounts this shrine. (Plates Nos. XXXVI and XXXVII.)

Between Nos. 19 and 20.—Pârvati placing her foot on the head of a buffalo. An attendant kneels on each side. Pârvati is armed with a dagger, trident, discus, and club in her right; and sword, conch, serpent, and axe in her left hands. On the left side of this space are worshipping figures of Bramhâ, an attendant and two *gandharvas*.

No. 20.—Śiva with twelve hands, each armed with the usual Śaivite emblems. On his right is an attendant, and four others are on his left. (Plate No. XXXVIII, Fig. 1.)

Between Nos. 20 and 21.—Nine devotees sit in contemplation, with an umbrella over each. The two figures on the extreme left side are Gaṇêśa and Śiva, armed with their several symbols. In continuation of these—but on the back—are the other seven; the first has—in the stone sculpture—been a female figure, but in the overlaid plaster work, two additional faces have been added, to convert it into Brahmâ. The next three, are female devotees; the others are—Nandikêśvara; a female; and the last, Śiva.

No. 21.—Śiva treading on Vyâdhi, the lord of sickness. The latter is on his back, with head hanging down; a three-headed *nâga* stretches its hoods over the recumbent figure; Śiva's axe rests on the back of the snake. Śiva has eight hands; in his right is a roll of beads. A small animal—resembling a cat—rests on the knees of the fallen Vyâdhi. (Plate No. XXXVIII, Fig. 2.)

Between Nos. 21 and 22.—A seated Śiva, with eight arms, holding snake, bell, trident, axe, etc.

No. 22.—Śiva, armed with the usual weapons, sits on the back of an elephant. A female devotee is in front. (Plate No. CXXIII, Fig. 1.)

Between Nos. 22 and 23.—A *yôgi* with four attendants.

No. 23.—Śiva—with Pârvati standing by his side, supports, and places in his hair, Ganga, the goddess of the river Ganges. (Plate No. CXXIII, Fig. 2.)

BETWEEN No. 23 AND SOUTH-WEST CORNER CELL.—Śiva and Pârvati with five attendants.

The last panel completes those on the south side of the court. The elevation of the complete group is given in Plate No. XXXVII.

CELLS ON THE WEST INNER SIDE OF THE COURT WALL.

Returning along the inner west side of the large court, and continuing from the south-west corner, the first space between the corner cell and No. 24 has—on the back—Śiva and Pârvati.

On the left side is Śiva, armed with his different weapons, dancing on a serpent; Pârvati stands near, and rests her hand on one of two kneeling *gandharvas*. (See Plate No. CXXIII, Fig. 3.)

No. 24.—Śiva, Pârvati, and child.

BETWEEN Nos. 24 AND 25.—Śiva, and Pârvati, with attendants.

No. 25.—Śiva, and Pârvati, with attendants, one of whom seems to be Brahmâ.

BETWEEN Nos. 25 AND 26.—Śiva and Pârvati.

No. 26.—Śiva, and Pârvati, with attendants.

BETWEEN Nos. 26 AND 27.—Śiva, and Pârvati, with attendants.

No 28.—Western doorway (built up). On one side is a *dvârapâla*; in the inner side are two *yâli* pillars somewhat different from those on the fronts of the cells; the figures on the piers, with hands clasped, kneel on a round lotus base; a five-hooded *nâga* is above each; and over it rests the pillar.

BETWEEN Nos. 28 AND 29.—Śiva and Pârvati.

No. 29.—Śiva and Pârvati.

BETWEEN Nos. 29 AND 30.—Śiva and Pârvati.

No. 30.—Śiva and Pârvati, with child and umbrella over.

BETWEEN Nos. 30 AND 31.—Śiva and Pârvati, with umbrella over.

No. 31.—Śiva, Parvati, child, and umbrella.

BETWEEN Nos. 31 AND 32.—Śiva and Pârvati, with umbrella.

No. 32.—Śiva, Pârvati, child, and umbrella.

BETWEEN No. 32 AND NORTH-WEST CORNER.—Śiva, Pârvati, child, and umbrella.

The above completes the panels on the west side. It will be observed that they are less varied than those before described.

CELLS ON THE NORTH SIDE OF THE COURT.

Returning along the north side, the space between the north-west corner recess, and No. 33, has the usual panel of Śiva and Pârvati seated.

No. 33.—Two figures of Śiva; one rests on an attendant with an axe over his shoulder; the figure on the right has his left foot resting on a platform. (Plate No. XXXIX, Fig. 1.)

BETWEEN Nos. 33 AND 34.—Pârvati under a tree, with attendant and *chaurie*.

No. 34.—Śiva and Pârvati seated by the side of a pillar. Three figures—one a devotee, and the others, two *gandharvas*, kneel under; one of the latter has a serpent, and the other a bow. (Plate No. XXXIX, Fig. 4.)

BETWEEN Nos. 34 AND 35.—Pârvati holding a parrot; an attendant is behind, and two elephants underneath.

No. 35.—Śiva seated in *yogâsana* under a banyan tree; his right leg rests on a deer; two *gandharvas* are held up on each side in his hands. Two *yôgis* kneel under. (Plate No. XL, Fig. 1.)

BETWEEN Nos. 35 AND 36.—Eleven *yôgis* are seated in a row on a platform; at each end of the group is a *yâḷi*.

On the right side is a panel with Pârvati under a tree, and *chaurie* bearer on each side.

No. 36.—Śiva in a kneeling posture; he has ten hands each armed with a different symbolical weapon. (Plate No. XL, Fig. 2.)

BETWEEN Nos. 36 AND 37.—Blank.

No. 37.—Is a large panel. The principal figure is Vishṇu, seated with a wife on each side; over are two attendants, who hold umbrellas, *chauries*, and symbols; on one side is a male, and on the other a female *dvârapâla*. Vishṇu seems to be seated in contemplation of Śiva, who is sculptured on a panel exactly opposite this one on the north wall of the *vimâna*. (Plate No. XLI, Fig. 1.)

BETWEEN Nos. 37 AND 38.—Śiva and Pârvati; on the left side is another Śaivite figure with five attendants.

No. 38.—Śiva as a *yôgi*, seated with Pârvati; two *gandharvas* support the pedestal on which they sit. Brahmâ sits on the left of the panel and aids in supporting the pedestal. Another figure, over Brahmâ, sits with hands crossed in contemplation. (Plate No. XLI, Fig. 2.)

BETWEEN Nos. 38 AND 39.—Pârvati playing on a *vîna*; a parrot is on the left side; attendant with *chaurie* on right, and two elephants underneath.

No. 39.—Śiva and Pârvati attended by two servants and a *gandharva*. (Plate No. CXXIII, Fig. 4.)

BETWEEN Nos. 39 AND 40.—Pârvati, holding in her left hand a flower, on which sits a parrot; an attendant is on her right, and a figure sits cross-legged under.

No. 40.—Śiva, Pârvati, and three attendants, supported on a lotus by Brahmâ. (Plate No. CXXIII, Fig. 5.)

BETWEEN Nos. 40 AND 41.—Śiva and Pârvati.

No. 41.—Śiva, Pârvati and two attendants, supported on a lotus by Vishṇu. Śiva has Brahmâ's head placed on the top of his own. An attendant of Vishṇu stands by, holding his conch and *chakra*. (Plate No. XLII, Fig. 1.)

BETWEEN Nos. 41 AND 42.—Pârvati, with attendant, parrot and two elephants.

No. 42.—Śiva, with Pârvati on his right. On the right of Pârvati are an attendant and *gandharva*. A female figure, probably Gaṅgâ, stands on Śiva's left hand. On the same side are Sûrya, Brahmâ, and a female with umbrella over. (Plate No. XLII, Fig. 2.)

BETWEEN Nos. 42 AND 43.—Pârvati, attendant and two deer under a tree.

No. 43.—Śiva, and Pârvati, with two *gandharvas* and two attendants. (Plate No. XXXIX, Fig. 3.)

BETWEEN Nos. 43 AND 44.—Śiva, and Pârvati, a halo—in plaster—is over Śiva's head.

No. 44.—Śiva dances, and supports a large five-hooded *nâga* with human head; the snake is coiled round his head. Underneath, are two dancing *gandharvas*. (Plate No. XXXIX, Fig. 5.)

BETWEEN Nos. 44 AND 45.—Pârvati, attendant, bird and two elephants.

No. 45.—Śiva and Pârvati seated; under, are two attendants—one standing, and the other kneeling. A *gandharva*, on the under side of Śiva's right, holds a mace, which extends up, and supports a *yâḷi* bearing a lotus, over which is a *gandharva* with a halo. (Plate No. XLIII, Fig. 1.)

BETWEEN Nos. 45 AND 46.—Pârvati, attendant, bird and two deer.

No. 46.—Śiva stands with his left foot raised, and resting on a pedestal; he holds a musical instrument across his body. Two devotees,—one with knotted hair, and the other bearded—stand on his left. Two bulls are seen—on the left of Śiva—ascending the sky, with Śiva and Pârvati on each. (Plate No. XLIII, Fig. 2.)

BETWEEN Nos. 46 AND 47.—Śiva and Pârvati.

No. 47.—Śiva seated on Nandikêśvara. Above, on each side, is a *gandharva*; and below, two attendants. (Plate No. XLIV, Fig. 1.)

BETWEEN Nos. 47 AND 48.—Pârvati with an attendant; a *yôgi* is underneath.

No. 48.—Śiva,—with Pârvati—placing Gaṅgâ on his head. A kneeling devotee supports another, who with uplifted hands is adoring Śiva. (Plate No. XLIV, Fig. 2.)

BETWEEN Nos. 48 AND 49.—Śiva and Pârvati.

No. 49.—Śiva, Pârvati and child; Brahmâ and Vishṇu, with *gandharvas* under, are worshipping the triad. (Plate No. XLV, Fig. 1.)

BETWEEN Nos. 49 AND 50.—Pârvati, attendant, bird and bull.

No. 50.—A standing Śaivite figure—six armed—is being worshipped by Brahmâ and Vishṇu. (Plate No. XLV, Fig. 2.)

BETWEEN Nos. 50 AND 51.—Śiva and Pârvati.

No. 51.—Śiva, as a *yôgi*, preaching to four devotees. Śiva has a beaded waist belt; and sandals with bead on each passing through between the toes.

The panel is entirely free of plaster, and the different details show the usual deep and bold cutting. (Plate No. XLVI, Fig. 1.)

BETWEEN Nos. 51 AND 52.—Pârvati, attendant, elephant and bird.

No. 52.—A large figure of Brahmâ supporting Hanumân in his left hand. Hanumân is worshipping a *liṅga*. (Plate No. XLVI, Fig. 2 and Plate No. XLVII.)

BETWEEN No. 52 and the north-east corner, is a seated figure of Śiva armed with a club.

In the north-east corner is an illegible inscription.

These complete the panels on the north side of the court.

EAST SIDE OF THE COURT.

Returning along the east side, from the north-east corner, the first space between that corner and No. 53 has a back panel with Śiva and Pârvati; also another with Śivá on the left side.

A detached Śaivite image stands in this space.

No. 53.—Śiva and Pârvati.

Space between Nos. 53 and 54.—Śiva and Pârvati.

No. 54.—Śiva and Pârvati.

BETWEEN Nos. 54 AND 55.—Śiva and Pârvati.

No. 55.—Śiva and Pârvati. (Plate No. XXXI.)

These panels complete the series on the interior sides of the large court and bring us to the right east entrance to the enclosure. This door has a *dvârapâla* on each side. A few of these figures have holes in their ears, evidently intended for the fixing of metal jewels; others also, probably have them, though they may be hidden under the plaster. This has been previously remarked on.

MAHÂMAṆḌAPAM.

This building stands in the east central portion of the large court. I have already shown (p. 11, F.N. 77) it originally stood detached from the central *vimâna*, though now a modern structure connects the two buildings. Some of the most strikingly archaic details in the entire temple are found in the *mahâmaṇḍapam*, these being the massive stone piers, with heavy square capitals (Plate No. XLVIII, Fig. 1), on one of which, is a later Châlukyan inscription (page 11).

The plan is a rectangle with the greater length from north to south. The four sides are open in the centre, and on each façade a portion of the wall is returned along the several elevations from the four corners. The east front has the entrance divided into three bays by two square piers, with a responding pilaster on the return wall at each side.

The west side—or back—is similarly divided, but the piers are octagonal for a portion of their length.

The north and south entrances are simple openings,—with pilasters on the sides,—undivided by piers. Inside, between these two doorways—extending north and south—are two rows of four piers each. These are octagonal for a portion of their length: the central space between the rows is equal to the breadth of the north and south doors; the four central piers of these rows are in a line east and west with the piers of the east and west openings; and the remaining central piers are severally in a line with the responding pilasters of the same openings. The ceiling of the *maṇḍapam* is thus divided into fifteen almost equal spaces.

The two square piers on the east front are in free stone; the left one has inscriptions on the front, sides and back; and the right pier an inscription on the front. All the piers are without bases. The capitals are of one design throughout, square, with great projection,—the extreme projecting mouldings of each, almost touching each other (see Plate XLVIII, Fig. 1). The details of the capitals are, a necking, large torus, cyma recta square abacus having rolls and band on the face, and brackets over. The two front piers are square throughout; the others have the lower portion square, the middle octagonal, and the upper portion—including the capital—square; all have a slight taper in their length. Exclusive of the two front piers, the others are granite; but the capitals and brackets in all cases are freestone. Several have circular lotus discs carved on the faces of the lower and upper square portions: these are identical with those on the piers of the north rock-cut cave at Mâmandûr.

The Châlukyan inscription—before referred to—is on the west face of the north pier on the west side next the *ardhamaṇḍapam*; it is considerably weatherworn but being deeply cut the letters are quite legible. It is at present completely protected by the east wall of the *ardhamaṇḍapam*, so the weather marks could only have been caused before the erection of the latter building.

The very design of the west opening shows it was never intended to be blocked up as it now is, but to present an open façade like that on the east.

Two *yâḷis* on the back responding pilasters are abutted against and partly covered by the east wall of the modern *ardhamaṇḍapam*.

The cornice in the compartments of the ceiling over the piers is a square moulding, with a projecting row of supporting *gandharvas* over; the ceiling itself is in flat stone slabs.

A perforated window in the east wall of the *ardhamaṇḍapam* opens into the *mahâmaṇḍapam*. It is much older than the building in which it now is, and has evidently been taken from some other place and built in where we now find it. The perforated work is a series of twisting boughs with openings between, partly filled by cross buds. Over the opening is a triple cornice with horse-shoe shaped panel; in it is a figure of Śiva, with eight arms; Pârvati is on his left, and Nandikêśvara on his right. On the circumference of the panel is a leaf ornament springing from *yâḷis* at the foot. (See Plate No. XLIX.)

Another window somewhat similar, is seen in the Kachêśvara temple. (See Plate No. CXXII.) It also, has evidently been removed from some other temple probably the Kailâsanâdha, and inserted in its present place. Both these are in a dark stone, and the panel in the former window is designed slightly after the style of some of the blackstone Châlukyan sculptures found in the Bellary District.

On the outside of the *mahâmaṇḍapam* the ground line is now on a level with the octagonal member of the basement. The mouldings above ground are similar to the base universally applied in other parts of the building: the upper square granite course is level with the floor. A Tamil inscription is cut on each of the faces of the base on the floor elevations; it returns along the back, but is blocked up by the east wall of the *ardha-maṇḍapam*, and only a few letters appear at each end.

On the east front—at the two corners of the return walls—are *yâḷis* with pilasters over. On each wall is a large panelled group, having a central niche with large Śaivite figure; and three lesser panels on each side, one over the other. The lowest of each of the side panels is a female *chaurie* bearer; the middle, a *gandharva* blowing a conch; and the upper, a *yâḷi* with rider. The crowning central feature, or pediment to each set of panels, is a figure or Gaṇapati with *yâḷis* and riders, and flowing floral ornament on each side of the upper central figure.

The main cornice which surmounts each façade and extends round the building, is of no great projection; over it, is a blocking course; and on the cornice are small pedimental horse-shoe niche ornaments—placed at intervals—with a figure in each. All are supported by a row of *gandharvas* under the cornice. Some fragments of a superstructure remain over the blocking course. These fragments are, I believe, the remains of a tower similar to that on the "Dharmarâja's" *ratha* at Mâmallâpuram, which this building otherwise resembles. The massive piers in the Kailâsanâdha *mahâmaṇḍapam* are evidently intended to support some great superincumbent weight, and this most probably was, or was intended to be, a tower similar to that at the *ratha* named. The arrangements of plan and design of the lower façades of the two examples are exactly similar; and the theory that the Kailâsa-nâdha *mahâmaṇḍapam* had a tower similar to the *ratha* is not improbable, and seems to be supported by what evidence there is on the subject. (See Plates Nos. XXVI and L.)

The south elevation has the same general design as the east side, but the figures in the panels vary; in the lower right panel, Lakshmî is seated on a lotus flower, holding lotus buds, conch and *chakra*. In the tier of minor panels on each side, are *chauries*, elephants, *gandharvas*, and attendants.

The large left panel on the same elevation has Pârvati seated with a noose in her right hand, and a lotus bud in her left. Two *chauries* and umbrellas are over; the other parts of the panels are the same as those on the right. (Plate No. XXVI.)

The north side of the same *maṇḍapam* has—in the large right panel—Pârvati seated with two attendants on her right; and on her left are a bird, and lamp bearers; the symbols she holds are broken; the side panels are similar to the others.

The large left panel is of bold and good design and deeply undercut; it represents Pârvati standing with her left foot on the back of the lion; she has sixteen hands, each armed with a different weapon.

This seems to have been a favourite subject with the sculptors, and the treatment is always good. This panel is very similar to, but larger than Nos. XXXII and XXIX. (See also No. LI, Fig. 2.)

ARDHAMAṆḌAPAM.

This building calls for only a passing notice; it is not contemporary with, or has any features in design common to the original building. The north and south walls are quite plain, without ornament of any kind; on the south side is a four-pillared raised verandah (see Plate No. XXVI), a ḍoor through which, enters the building. The east wall is built close to, and covers the sculptures that undoubtedly exist on the west wall of the *mahâmaṇḍapam*: a perforated window in the wall opens into the latter building. The inside is divided by two rows of six slender pillars of Vijianagar date. (See Plate No. XXIV and Fig. 2 in XXXIX). Several old inscribed stones are built into the floor and ceiling of the building. The principal shrine enters off the west end of the *ardhamaṇḍapam*. On each side of the shrine entrance is a chamber; these two are the original recesses—similar to those on the exterior of the *vimâna*—between the north-east, and south-east corner shrines, and the east entrance to the great central shrine. Originally they would be visible from the outside; and the weatherworn appearance of their sculptures shows they have been. In the right recess—on the back wall,—is a four-armed Śiva dancing: below, are his attendants; the minor panel on his right has Vishṇu; and on the left panel is Brahmâ, both worshipping. (Plate No. LI, Fig. 1.)

The left side of the recess has Pârvati on the lion, with attendants, and *gandharvas* on each side. The right side is covered with masonry.

The left recess has panels similar to the other, with Śiva and minor worshipping deities on the back; Pârvati is on the right side of the recess, and the left is blocked up with masonry. This is a portion of that forming the north and south walls of the *ardhamaṇḍapam*. The panels blocked up, are those on the south side of the north-east corner shrine, and those on the north side of that at the south-east corner.

On the right side of the entrance to the main shrine containing the Kailâsanâdha *liṅga*, is a *dvârapâla*. On the back interior wall of the shrine, is a panel with seated figures of Śiva, Pârvati and child. Some brass figures are used on festival occasions. (Plate No. LII, Fig. 3.)

The *vimâna* has the principal shrine in the centre; on the exterior is a lesser one at each corner; and another on each face, except the east, where the entrance to the central shrine is, and has always been. It now enters through the *ardhamaṇḍapam*, but before that building was erected, the entrance would be through the porch—similar to the exterior *vimâna* shrines—direct from the open, and up a flight of steps.

Around the *vimâna*, and in the recesses formed by the projecting exterior shrines, are a series of *nandis* placed on the ground, and facing the different quarters. (See Plates Nos. XXIV and XXVI.) The identity of this idea with that at the Mâmallâpuram "shore" temple has been noted (p. 20).

At each of the corners formed by the projecting shrines and extending around the *vimâna*, is a series of triple *yâḷis* and riders, intended to represent a support and guard to the temple.

In describing the panels on the exterior ground storey of the *vimâna*, it will be convenient to adopt a course similar to that used in noting those on the courtyard cells. Commencing, therefore, with the panels in the south-east corner shrine,—which enters on the east side,—the back panel represents a large kneeling figure of Śiva—with eight arms—holding the usual weapons, noose, trident, sword, serpent and others undistinguishable.

On the left side is Brahmâ paying homage; under him, are two *gandharvas*, and what seems like a mountain with a figure seated on it, is on his left: two *gandharvas* are on his upper left side.

On the right side of the shrine is Vishṇu and attendants, also worshipping Śiva; the panel is too much weatherworn for the details to be made out. (Plates Nos. LI and LIII to LXII.)

On the south exterior side of this shrine is a four-armed Śiva, with Pârvati. Beneath Śiva, are *gandharvas*, and over, an elephant. Above, is a small panel with an eight-armed Śiva and *gandharva*. (Plate No. XXVI and Plates Nos. LI and LIII to LXII.)

On the south exterior wall of the central shrine, and in the space between the south-east corner shrine and that on the middle of the south side, are a six-armed Śiva, and Pârvati, seated with their feet on Vyâdhî the god of sickness.

The panel on the right side of the same recess is supported on *yâḷis*, and represents Lakshmî, with lotus buds. On the top, are *gandharvas* surrounded by a finely-cut floral ornament. (Plates Nos. XXVI, LI and LIII to LXII.)

On the left side of the same recess is the entrance to the shrine on the centre of the south façade of the *vimâna*. On the left side of the door is a *dvârapâla*; over, are eleven *śishyas*. In the shrine—on the back—is Śiva seated with his left foot on a *gandharva*; the platform on which he sits is supported by two *yâḷi* pillars. Brahmâ and Vishṇu are in attendance, worshipping. On the left interior side, is Śiva—in bridegroom's dress—seated on a bull, with attendants; a *gandharva* leads the animal.

On the right side of the shrine is Pârvati seated on a pedestal supported by a *yaḷi* on the left, and two *gandhârvas*. She is shown dressed as a bride. The two panels seemingly represent the marriage of Śiva and Pârvati.

On the south outside face of this shrine is Śiva as a *yôgi* seated under a tree; he has four arms; in one of his left is a torch; beside him are birds, two deer and a snake under. The panel is supported on an elephant's head. The side panels have *yôgis* under, with *yâḷis* and ornament on top. (Plates Nos. XXVI and LXII.)

The west exterior side of the shrine has Vishṇu seated with his foot on a pedestal; he and his attendants are worshipping Śiva who is shown on the next panel.

The panel referred to, on the back of the recess formed by the shrine on the centre of the south façade of the *vimâna*, and that at the south-west corner, is an exceedingly fine one; it shows Śiva standing in a diamond-shaped recess; he has eight arms, which hold, in his right, serpent, axe, and noose; and in his left a large trident and other symbols; he wears the sun as a crown. The lesser panels adjacent to this central one, are occupied by various minor worshipping deities, with Brahmâ and others on the left, Vishṇu and *gandharvas* on the right. Śiva is supported by Vishṇu, in his *varâha avatâr*, with two hands resting on the ground, and other two holding the conch and discus. (Plates Nos. XXVI and LXI.)

The left side of the recess is occupied by worshipping attendants.

The shrine at the south-west corner has, in the panel on the south exterior side, Śiva as a beggar, with sandals on his feet; two females and *Yôgi* are worshipping. The whole is supported on an elephant's head. The panel over, has a ten-armed Śiva, each hand with a symbol.

The south-west corner shrine enters from the west. The panel on the back of the interior is similar to that on the left side of the porch of the Mahêṇḍravarma shrine. It shows a Śaivite figure—considerably larger than life size; he has matted hair, and carries a cloud banner, and three-hooded *nâga*; with trident and axe on his right, and a sun on his left. A female stands on each side, probably Pârvati, and Lakshmî. (Plate No LXI.)

The right interior side of the shrine has a panel with three male attendants; and the left side, three females with a cornice over.

The first space on the west side of the *vimâna*, between the south-west corner shrine, and the one on the centre of the west elevation, has Śiva kneeling on a platform; a three-hooded snake is coiled round his right leg. He has ten arms; in his right are trident, drum, noose, and one supports a long thin shaft, which extends up on the right, into what looks like a *chaurie*,—but may be a cloud banner,—and goes behind the figure, right across the panel. In the left hands, are axe, torch, serpent, and another symbol somewhat like a skull. Three dancing *gandharvas*, armed with swords, are under. The minor panel on the right has Pârvati with her foot resting on a bull; two *gandharvas* are over. The minor left panel has a figure with a crown seated on two *gandharvas*, one of whom plays a flute and the other a conch: an attendant is in the upper right side of the panel.

The group is supported on an elephant's head. (Plate No. LI.)

On the right side of this recess is an eight-armed dancing Śiva. On the left side of the same recess is Gaṇapati, with two *gandharvas* over. A female attendant stands in a panel on his left.

The shrine in the centre of the west side of the *vimâna* enters from the west side. It shows—on the back of the interior—a large figure of Śiva, with six arms, and Pârvati. Śiva holds in his right hands a dog, garland of skulls and serpent; a *chaurie*—bearing *gandharva* is under. The upper left hands support Gaṅgâ, and an elephant's skin. The left foot rests on an attendant. (Plate No. LIX.)

On the right side of this shrine is Vishṇu armed with conch and discus; some attendants wait on him. The left side of the shrine has two attendants.

In the back of the recess between the centre shrine on the west façade of the *vimâna*, and the shrine at the north-west corner, is an eight-armed Śiva dancing, with Nandikêśvara on his left, and a small *gandharva* on his right; Śiva has a *nâga* coiled round his neck. The *gandharva* is completely free of plaster, and shows very minute carving, the eyes, eyebrows, and teeth in the mouth are all cut in the stone. The lesser panel on the right of the central one, has Vishṇu; in the panel on the left is Brahmâ. (Plate No. LVIII. See also Nos. LI, and LIII to LXII).

On the right side of the recess is Śiva seated on a platform, supported by a *gandharva*. A long musical instrument rests across the left shoulder, and a serpent across the right.

The sculpture represents Śiva as Arddhanârîśvara, (half male and female). A female attendant occupies each side panel.

On the left side of the recess, a worshipper—holding a three-hooded serpent—sits on a mountain. They are supported by two *gandharvas* playing the flute and conch.

The shrine at the north-west corner of the *vimâna*, has, in the back interior panel, an eight-armed Śiva seated on a chariot, drawn by two horses; the heads of the horses, and front of the vehicle are shown towards the front, with a wheel on each side. (Plate No. LIII. See also Nos. LI and LIII to LXII.)

The right side of the shrine, is occupied by a tier of two panels—five figures above, and seven below. The left wall has five figures in the upper half, and six in the lower. On the north exterior side of the north-west corner shrine is Śiva crushing Vyâdhi; above is a panel with two Śaivite figures. (Plate No. LIV.)

On the north wall of the *vimâna*, in the recess between the north-west corner shrine, and that on the centre of the north face, is Śiva and Pârvati. Śiva has eight arms, and various symbols, including noose, bow, and umbrella: three dancing *gandharvas* are under.

The minor panel on the right, shows Pârvati seated on a lion. That on the left shows Lakshmî seated on a pedestal. A lion supports the group. (Plate No. LV, Fig. 1.)

On the left side of the recess is Śiva as a beggar; an attendant and *yâḷi* are in panels on each side.

On the north side of the central shrine, on the north façade of the *vimâna*, is Śiva in *yogâsana* seated over a *bhûta*: these are supported on an elephant. The lower side panels have worshipping figures of Brahmâ on Śiva's right; and Vishṇu on his left. In the two upper side panels are a *yâḷi* and rider. (No. LV, Fig. 2. See also Nos. LIII to LXVIII.)

The shrine in the centre of the north side of the *vimâna* enters from the east. Inside, is a granite platform for an image, with basement and cornice moulding. The panel on the back interior is the same as that in the centre shrine on the south façade of the *vimâna*. It represents Śiva supported by *gandharvas*, and *yâḷis*, with worshipping figures of Brahmâ, and Vishṇu. The panels on the two interior sides are the same as those on the shrine referred to.

The recess on the north façade, between the north centre and north-east shrines, shows—on the back panel—Pârvati on a lion; the design is similar to those of the same subject already noted. She has ten arms; and carries an umbrella, with trident, noose, and sword in her right hands; one of the lower right rests on her thigh; the other is shown in *abhayahasta*. The left hands hold an axe, shield and serpent, while two other hands grasp and bend a long bow. She is ornamented with jewels on wrists, ankles, etc. The smaller panel on the left of the central one has a stout figure of Pârvati; over her right is Nandikêśvara; on her left is a female attendant. The lesser panel on the right of the larger, has Pârvati—in this instance, represented with a slender waist—seated on a pedestal supported by a pillar. On her right is Simhâ; on her left, what appears to be a bull. (Plate No. LVI and Nos. LIII to LVII.)

On the left side of the recess is a *dvârapâla*.

On the north exterior side of the shrine at the north-east corner of the *vimâna*, are Śiva and Pârvati. Śiva has four arms, and rests one foot on a lotus. Two of his hands hold the elephant's skin over his crown.

The shrine enters from the east, and inside is a *pîṭham* for an image. The back and side panels are the same as those in the corresponding shrine on the south side of the *vimâna* *i.e.*, a kneeling Śiva, worshipped on the side panels by Brahmâ and Vishṇu.

These complete the sculptured panels around the exterior of the *vimâna*.

VIMÂNA TOWER.

The basement is formed of a granite sub-base; carved "*gandharva*" plinth, ornamented semi-octagonal base, small carved "elephant" blocks, in freestone; and sur-base in granite with Pallava Grantha inscriptions. (See Plates Nos. XXVI and LIV.)

In the recesses formed by the exterior shrines are the series of *nandis* already noted. These are large, and each cut out of a single block of freestone. The walls above the base, are covered with the sculptured panels just described. At each of the angles of the walls, and on each side of the panels are pilasters; those on the corners have *yâlis*.

The general elevation of the superstructure, is a small tower over each of the exterior shrines at the corners and façades; the *śikharas* over those at the corners are square; over those on the façades, they are semi-barrel shaped. Above these, on the main tower, is a storey with a series of two weather-worn sculptured panels, on each face of the central projection, and one at each corner; pilasters are at the corners. Over this, is a double cornice, with small *śikharas*; the storeys above are successively stepped back, forming a slight platform between each. The *śikharas* over the double cornice mentioned, are one on each face, and one at each corner. Over this, is a square portion with cornice, a *nandi* at each corner, a seated figure on each front,[100] and a finial over. (Plate No. XXVI.) The tower is capped by an octagonal *śikhara* with small pediment on each front.

The whole tower is plastered over, but except in some of the details of the sculptures, there is no doubt but that the original design has been faithfully followed in the covering process. In many places where the plaster has been detached, but still partly adhering, the underlying stonework is generally the same as the plaster which covers it. The principal difference between the plaster and the stone is, that, where sculptures have been covered, the plaster work is much coarser in its execution, and only attempts to reproduce in outline or in a general way, the design of the stone sculpture underneath. The stone carvings are, without exception, beautifully and minutely chiselled, whereas, when these have been covered over, the small details of jewels or other ornaments have only been imitated by rough incisions in the wet plaster by a knife or some such instrument. The design and treatment of the various details of the tower are identical in style with similar features at the "Dharmarâja's" and other *rathas* at Mâmallâpuram. There is an archaic peculiarity above these and other works of a like date, not to be mistaken.

---

[100] At the Mâmallâpuram "shore" temple, these *nandis* are replaced by figures playing conches. The *nandis* are shown on all the Kâñchi Pallava temples.

VAIKUṆṬHA PERUMÂḶ TEMPLE, KÂÑCHÎPURAM.

This building stands at the other end of the town, almost due east from the Kailâsanâdha temple, and a few hundred yards west from the Kâñchîpuram railway station.

In size, archæological and architectural importance, it is—of the group of Pallava temples—second to the Kailâsanâdha. The most important and interesting feature in the building is the *vimâna* tower (see Plate No. LXIII), which bears a distinct resemblance to the ancient *vihâras*.[101]

This *vimâna* has a tier of three shrines, one over the other.[102]

The lowest shrine is surrounded by three walls and two covered *prâkâras*. The first or inner shrine wall encloses the three shrines through being carried right up above the ceiling of the uppermost one. The second wall encloses the covered first *prâkâras* of the first and second upper shrines and forms an open platform round the third shrine. The third wall encloses the second covered *prâkâra* of the first shrine, is carried up and forms an open platform round the second shrine.

The general plan (Plate No. LXIV) is the shrine with double *prâkâras*, enclosed in a courtyard with a covered verandah on the four sides. The shrine enters from the east through an *ardhamaṇḍapam*. On the east side of the courtyard is the *mahâmaṇḍapam* entirely roofed over, and open on its east and west sides only; a modern addition has been added to the front façade leaving a door only, open on that side. Some distance to the east, is an unfinished Vijayanagar *gôpuram*; it is only carried up to the ceiling of the entrance door. On the external sides of the entrance is a raised platform, with a six-pillared verandah; two panels on the exterior are shown in No. LXV. To the west of the *gôpuram*—between it, and the entrance to the temple through the *mahâmaṇḍapam*—are a small shrine, *pîṭham*, and *dhvajastambam*.

The exterior of the courtyard wall is divided into bays by *yâli* pilasters, with pinnacles surmounting the wall. In the bays are niches, with carved pedimental ornament over. A moulded base surrounds the sides, and the wall head is capped by a double moulded cornice, with carved blocks and moulded blocking course over. (See Plates Nos. LXVI and LXVII.)

The treatment of design in the niches is similar to those on cave No. 21, at Mâmallâpuram.

The eastern wing of the *mahâmaṇḍapam* is comparatively modern; its piers are somewhat plain and of ordinary design. A small panel in the same building, and one of the piers are shown on Plate No. LXVIII, Figs. 1 and 2. On the inner sides of the building are a series of six enclosed and two open chambers; these divisions are simply formed by stone and mud walls.

The *ardhamaṇḍapam* is attached to, and is the porch through which the shrine is entered. It has eight *yâli* piers, and four pilasters of a distinctive Pallava type. On the east side of the inner shrine wall is a panel, (Plate No. LXIX, Fig. 1), and others on the north and south sides of the second shrine wall. (Nos. LXX and Fig. 2 in LXIX.) The external *prâkâra* walls of the shrine, and *ardhamaṇḍapam* are also panel sculptured. The upper portion of the tower is also similarly ornamented; the details of the several panels

---

101 See Fergusson: *Ind. and Eas. Arch.*, p. 134, pl. 67.

102 This arrangement is identical with that at the "*Dharmarâja's Ratha*" in Mâmallâpuram.

will be seen on the different sheets, and their position—on the elevations, (see Fig. 1 in plate LXIX and plates LXXI, LXXII, Fig. 3 in LXIX, LXXIII, LXXIV, LXXV, LXXVI, LXXVII, LXXVIII, LXXIX, LXXX, LXXXI, LXXXII, LXXXIII, LXXXIV, and LXXXV. On the base of the *vimâna*, are inscriptions in Tamil and Sanskrit. In the first shrine is a large seated figure of Vishṇu (Plate No. LXXXIV; in the second shrine is a reclining figure of the same deity (Plate No. LXXXVI) with others: and there is also another in the third shrine. The second and third shrines enter from the east side, off the platforms which surround the tower at the different stages. The tower is ascended by a stone stair; and is built of stone, plastered over.

The verandah surrounding the inner sides of the courtyard has thirty-four *yâḷi* piers similar to those in the *ardhamaṇḍapam.* (Plate No. LXXXVII.)

On the inner walls of the court is a continuous series of stone sculptured panels, representing scenes—evidently from one of the *purânas*, but which, it is difficult to say. The general grouping of the whole, and style of the figures themselves, are very similar to those on the sculptured frescoes of "Arjuna's penance," and the other unfinished bas-relief near by, at Mâmallâpuram. (See Plates Nos. LXXXVIII to XCII.) The type of the figures seems very archaic, and some representations of temples resemble the "Bhima's" "Dharmarâjah's" and other *rathas* at Mâmallâpuram. Through the action of the temple priests in refusing admittance, to even the outer precincts, to a non-Hindu, a description of the panels from the originals cannot be given; such information therefore, as may be required about these and other details of the interior, can only be had by a reference to the drawings.

MÂTAṄGÊŚVARA TEMPLE, KÂÑCHÎPURAM.

This temple stands in the fields west from the hospital, and south-west from the Vaikuṇṭha Perumâḷ temple. There are no remains of a courtyard; and the plan is simply a small shrine with massive walls, and entrance through a pillared porch on the west side. (Plate No. XCIII.) In this respect the plan is similar to that of the Kailâsanâdha *vimâna*. The side and back walls of the porch and shrine have a series of panels on each. (See Fig. 4 in LXXIV and Plates Nos. XCIV to XCVI and fig. 2 in XCVII.)

The shrine contains a black stone *liṅga*. Over it is the tower, which is hollow, with each successive course corballed over that immediately below it. The porch has four piers of the Pallava type, (Plates Nos. XCVIII and XCIX), each with a lion base, the tail of the lion being curved up the back of the pillar, similar to that on the curious *yâḷi* shrine discovered during the excavations at the "shore" temple at Mâmallâpuram in 1884. Over the lion—on the piers—is an ornamental band with polygonal-sided necking, large projecting capital and a square abacus over. An inscription of a few letters is on each of the two front piers. The brackets over the pillars have filleted rolls, with upright ornamental band on each face; responding pilasters are on each side. Similar piers are common at the Seven Pagodas, and at some of the other Kâñchîpuram temples, but none are found at the Kailâsanâdha temple. The pillars under note, compared with those at the latter temple, show an advancement in the period of the style.

The back of the porch has pilasters responding to the detached piers, with figured panels on each side. (Plate No. XCV.) The ceiling is flat, with plain filleted and roll cornice. Between the two rear pillars is a small *nandi*; another, slightly larger, stands on the ground in front of the temple.

Around the exterior is a sub-base with plain panels; a square granite moulding is over; and sur-base, with plain and octagonal mouldings completes the basement: the upper member is a granite slab.

The walls over, are divided by pilasters, placed at intervals; those at the corners have *yâḷis* and riders. The north and east walls have Śaivite single figure-sculptured panels between the pilasters; the south wall has the spaces for the figures uncarved.

There are two niches on the exterior sides and back, and one on each of the exterior sides of the porch. Sculptured floral ornaments surmount the niches; but those on the back, and some on the sides are uncarved, or only partly so. (Plate No. C.)

The cornice over, has small carved blocks at intervals, similar to other cornices before described.

The tower is square, and built in three storeys, with circular surmounting *śikhara* and *kalaśa*. (Plates Nos. CIX and C.)

The whole building is in stone, with comparatively little plaster remaining.

MUKTÊŚVARA TEMPLE, KÂÑCHÎPURAM.

This shrine stands north from the Mâtaṅgêśvara, and north-west from the Vaikuntha Perumâḷ temples.

The Muktêśvara, and Mataṅgêśvara temples are in most respects, almost exactly similar.

The shrine is square, with thick walls, and a four-pillared entrance porch on the west side. (Plate No. CI.) The two front piers in the porch, are of the *yâḷi* form; the two back, are cylindrical. (Plate No. CII.)

In the shrine is a black stone *liṅga.* The inner side, and back walls of the porch and shrine, have Śaivite sculptured panels. (Plates Nos. CIII to CV and Fig. 1 in XCVII.)

A tower, similar to that on the Mataṅgêśvara temple, rises over the shrine. (Plates Nos. CVI and CVII.)

The external walls of the porch and shrine are divided by pilasters, and sculptured with single figures. (Plate No. CVII.)

The base is similar to that on the other temple mentioned, and has inscriptions in Pallava Tamiḷ.

A small *piṭham*, and *nandi maṇḍapam* stand in front. (Fig. 4 in Plate No. LXIX.)

TRIPURÂNTAKÊŚVARA TEMPLE, KÂÑCHÎPURAM.

This is a small shrine in one of the streets between the Kachêśvara, and great Śiva temple.

The shrine is square, and, like the other ancient temples under note, is enclosed by very thick walls (Plate No. CVIII); the cell contains a *liṅga*; the floor of the porch and shrine is several feet above the ground level.

On the east side of the shrine is the porch, and,—blocking up its east entrance,—an unsightly modern brick *maṇḍapam* erected without any attempt at the introduction of architectural features.

The original plan has been similar to, but slightly smaller than the two temples just before described; that is, with a shrine and pillared porch only.

On the interior back wall of the shrine is a sculptured panel (Fig. 1 in plate No. LII); and others are on the sides and back of the porch (Nos. CIX and CX). These are very spirited in their grouping and execution, and their identity in period and style with those on the other Pallava examples is at once evident: they represent scenes from the Śaivite *purâṇa*.

The porch has sufficient projection to admit of two front piers only; the present supports are modern; the originals were most likely *yâḷi* piers, but they have disappeared. Some *yâḷi* bases lying in the courtyard of the Pâṇḍavaperumâḷ temple—at no great distance from this one—have no connection with the temple in which they now are; these may probably have been the originals of the Tripurântakêśvara porch. (Fig. 4 in plate No. LII.)

The brick *maṇḍapam*, with its floor line close to the ground level, calls for no special remark, except as to the contrast it offers to the ancient building to which it is attached. It only serves as an example of the degeneracy of some modern Hindu constructive work. It must be much less than a century old, if even that.

The base surrounding the old temple, is the same as those round the two previously described temples; on its usual upper square granite course are inscriptions in Pallava Tamiḷ. The walls are built of a soft reddish freestone—identical with that used at the Kailâsanâtha temple. It has suffered severely from the weather; and the resulting hollows in the sculptures have been filled in with bricks and plaster; the portions remaining intact, are however, distinct in their Pallava character. The interior panels are particularly good and in complete preservation, and leave no doubt as to their classification.

The external walls of the porch and shrine are covered with sculptured panels. (Nos. CXI, CXII.)

The *vimâna* is evidently built in stone, though now plastered over. At each of the four corners of the top of the tower next the *śikhara*, is the usual *nandi*; and other two over the front wall of the porch. (Plate No. CXIII.) Inside the *maṇḍapam*, are two figures of Gaṇêśa, and Thandakêśvara. (Plate No. CXIV.)

A *nandi maṇḍapam* with *pîṭhams* stand on the east side.

Around the modern courtyard are some recent brick erections, undeserving of notice.

The details of the architecture would seem to show this temple,—particularly the tower —slightly later in date than the others.

AIRÂVATÊŚVARA TEMPLE, KÂÑCHÎPURAM.

Is close to the north entrance of the Kachêśvara temple, and is the smallest and most incomplete of the Pallava examples in Kâñchîpuram.

The plan is a shrine with simple unpillared porch (Plate No. CXV), having its entrance from the west.

The panels on the interior back and sides of the shrine, and those on the sides of the porch are in fairly good preservation, and are Śaivite in character. (Plates Nos. CXVI, CXVII and figs. 1, 2 and 3 in plate No. CXVIII.)

The panels on the exterior are almost entirely worn away and filled in with brickwork and plaster; those in anything like good preservation are shown in Plate No. CXIX. The striking similarity of the style of these, to some at the Kailâsanâdha temple, is quite apparent.

The base surrounding the building is the usual one. There are no remains of a tower over the shrine.

This temple is small, with few of its details remaining thoroughly intact, but the architectural and sculptural features that do still exist, show its Pallava origin.

This completes the list of known existing Pallava structural temples in the once capital city of Southern India.

Mention has been however made of the examples remaining at Tiruppadikuṇram near Kâñchîpuram, and Kûram in the same district.

The first of these is a small building with few architectural details, and no sculptures worthy of note. A peculiarity about it, due to modern additions, is the blocking up of the original shrine on the ground floor, and constructing another in the upper storey of the tower with a stair leading up to it. The temple seems of late Pallava date.

PERUMÂḶ TEMPLE, KÛRAM.

This temple is situated 9 miles north-north-west of Kâñchîpuram.

The original plan has been comprised in a shrine and porch only. This has been the usual arrangement in all these temples; and any other accessory buildings were always built detached from the central shrine.

A *maṇḍapam* and open porch, with small shrine, *dhvajastambam*, and *pîṭhams* have been added in the Vijayanagar period. (Plate No. CXX.)

For present purposes the original building only, need be noted.

A slight resemblance to the characteristics of Pallava architecture presents itself in the building, but in an advanced period of the style; in fact, such as would almost seem to place the temple at an early Chôḷa period.

The basement is different from those universally seen in the Kâñchîpuram examples, and follows more after some temples of obvious Chôḷa date,—such as Manimaṅgalam, Tennêri, etc. The continuous sculptured panels on the exterior walls are wanting, and their place is filled by a single niche on each of the façades, again resembling the Chôḷa temples noted. The panels on the interior of the porches, and shrines of the early temples have no existence here.

The *yâḷis* at the corners are a connecting link between late Pallava, and early Chôḷa architecture; and we see them here, though in a form slightly modified from those of earlier examples.

The blocks on the cornice again, have lost the distinctive horse-shoe form, universal at Mâmallâpuram and Kâñchîpuram; and the later leaf ornament under, replaces the row of *gandharvas* seen on the others.

The tower wants the pyramidal massiveness peculiar to early Pallava architecture, and its more elongated form is an advance in this respect, on that at the Kâñchîpuram Tripurânta-kêśvara.

The *nandis* on the upper storeys are replaced by figures of Garuḍa. (Plate No. CXXI.)

The evidence of the copperplate,[103] formerly in possession of the temple, but now in the Madras Museum, would seem to place this building in the list of Pallava examples. It is, however, a very doubtful specimen, and, if in reality Pallava, must be one of the very latest examples. It may have been commenced by the Pallavas and completed by the Chôḷas, though the lower members of the basement—being different from the usual form—would not seem even to support this view.

A very considerable period must have elapsed between the completion of the Kâñchîpuram temples, and the foundation of this one; and, in the interval, the distinctive features of the early Pallava would be merging into the Chôḷa style: this may account for the change.

Everything therefore, seems to point to the temple being of a transitional period in the two styles of architecture.

---

[103] *South Ind. Ins.*, Vol. I, pp. 144 and 155.

PLATE I.

Photogravure.

Survey of India Offices Calcutta, October 190[illegible]

SOUTH EAST VIEW OF KAILÂSANÂDHA TEMPLE.

KÂNCHÎPURAM

PLATE II

Photogravure.

Survey of India Offices, Calcutta, October [illegible]

NORTH-EAST VIEW OF KAILĀSANĀDHA TEMPLE.

KĀÑCHĪPURAM

PLATE III.

Photogravure. Survey of India Offices, Calcutta, October 1903.

NORTH-EAST VIEW OF KAILÂSANÂDHA TEMPLE.

KÂÑCHÎPURAM.

Photogravure.

Survey of India Offices Calcutta, November 1903.

BACK VIEW OF KAILĀSANĀDHA TEMPLE.

KĀÑCHĪPURAM.

PLATE V

Photogravure. Survey of India Offices Calcutta, November, 1909.

VIEW OF SECOND MAIN ENTRANCE GOPURAM, KAILÂSANÂDHA TEMPLE,
KÂÑCHÎPURAM.

Photogravure

Survey of India Offices, Calcutta, November [illegible]

SOUTH CORRIDOR FROM THE EAST AND PORTION OF MAIN SHRINE, KAILĀSANĀDHA TEMPLE,

KĀÑCHIPURAM.

PLATE VII.

Photogravure. Survey of India Offices Calcutta, November 190[illegible]

WEST CORRIDOR FROM THE SOUTH AND PORTION OF MAIN SHRINE, KAILÂSANÂDHA TEMPLE, KÂÑCHÎPURAM.

PLATE VIII

Photogravure

Survey of India Offices Calcutta, November, [illegible]

NORTH CORRIDOR FROM THE WEST AND PORTION OF MAIN SHRINE, KAILÂSANÂDHA TEMPLE,

KÂÑCHÎPURAM.

PLATE IX

Photogravure

Survey of India Offices Calcutta, [illegible]

NORTH CORRIDOR FROM THE EAST, AND PORTION OF MAIN SHRINE, KAILÂSANÂDHA TEMPLE,
KÂÑCHÎPURAM.

Photogravure. Survey of India Offices Calcutta, November 1903.

VIEW OF MAIN SHRINE, KAILÁSANÁDHA TEMPLE,
KÁÑCHÎPURAM.

PLATE XI

Photogravure

Survey of India Offices, Calcutta, November, [illegible]

PIERS IN THE FRONT MANDAPAM, KAILASANADHA TEMPLE,
KÂÑCHÎPURAM.

Photogravure.

Survey of India Offices Calcutta, November [illegible]

PANELS ON THE BACK OF THE GARBHAGRIHAM, KAILÂSANÂDHA TEMPLE, KÂÑCHIPURAM.

Photogravure.

Survey of India Offices, Calcutta, November 1888

PANELS ON THE NORTH SIDE OF THE GARBHAGRIHAM, KAILÁSANÂDHA TEMPLE, KÁÑCHÍPURAM.

PLATE XIV.

Photogravure. Survey of India Offices, Calcutta, December 1908.

SOUTH-WEST VIEW OF VAIKUNTHA PERUMÂL TEMPLE,
KÂNCHÎPURAM.

PLATE XV

Photogravure

Survey of India Offices, Calcutta, December 1912.

SOUTH-EAST VIEW OF VAIKUNTHA PERUMÂL TEMPLE,
KÂNCHÎPURAM.

PLATE XVI.

Photogravure

Survey of India Offices, Calcutta, December 1908

SOUTH-WEST VIEW OF MATANGÉSVARA TEMPLE,

KÁÑCHÎPURAM.

PLATE XVII

Photogravure

Survey of India Offices, Calcutta, December [illegible]

SOUTH-EAST VIEW OF MATANGĒŚVARA TEMPLE,

KĀÑCHĪPURAM.

PLATE XVIII.

Photogravure. Survey of India Offices, Calcutta, December 1909.

SOUTH-WEST VIEW OF MUKTĒSVARA TEMPLE,

KĀÑCHĪPURAM.

PLATE XIX.

Photogravure

Survey of India Offices, Calcutta, December 1903.

SOUTH EAST VIEW OF MUKTESVARA TEMPLE.

KÃÑCHĪPURAM.

Photogravure.

Survey of India Offices, Calcutta, December 1903.

NORTH WEST VIEW OF TRIPURĀNTAKEŚVARA TEMPLE.

KĀÑCHĪPURAM.

KACHÊŚVARA TEMPLE. PLATE XXI.

TWO PILLER BASES AT ÂDITYA-TIRTHA TANK.

KAÑCHÎPURAM.

FIG. 1.

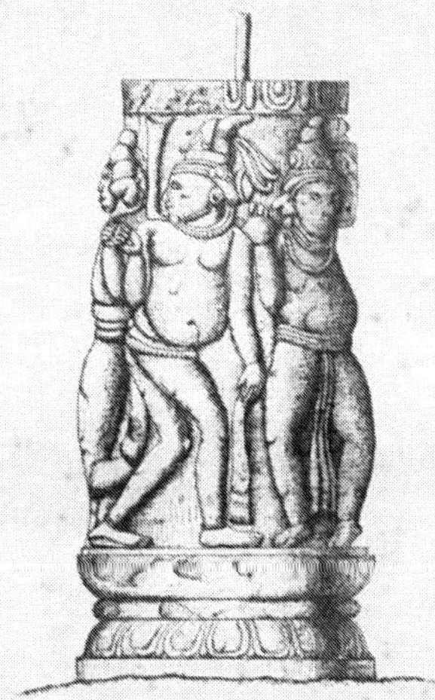

FIG. 2.

Scale of 12 1 2 3 4 Feet.

PLATE XXII

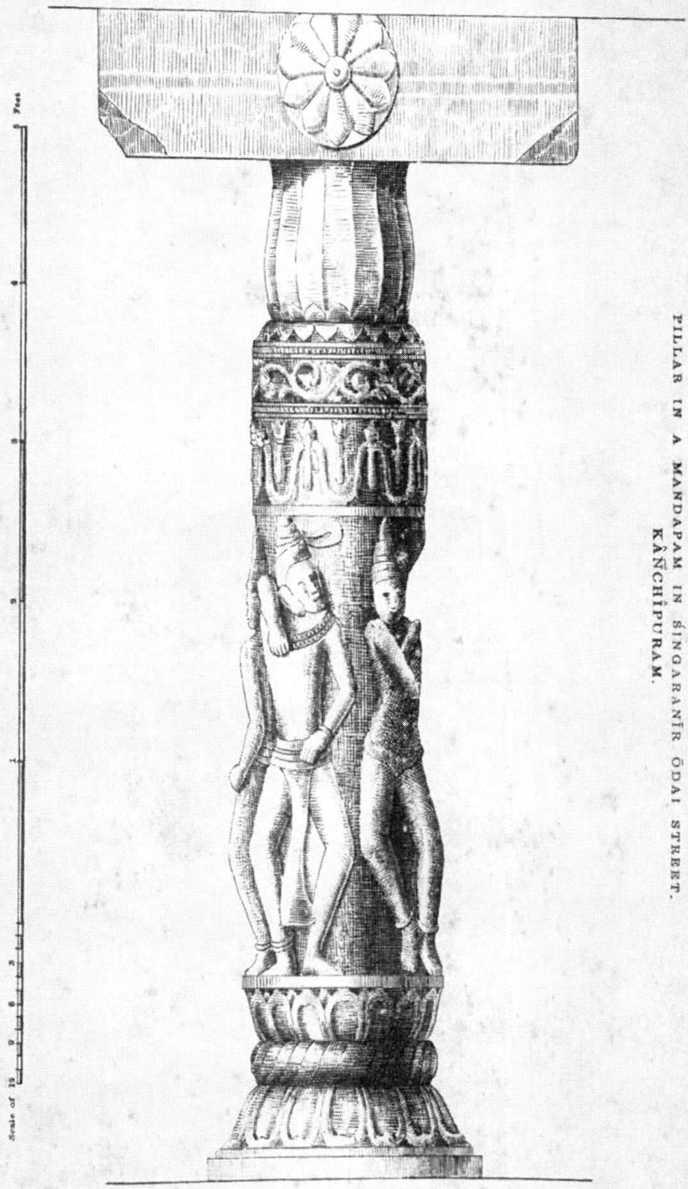

PILLAR IN A MANDAPAM IN ŚINGARANĪR ŌDAI STREET,
KÂÑCHÎPURAM.

PLATE XXIII.

KACHÊŚVARA TEMPLE.

BASES AT THE TANK,

KÂÑCHÎPURAM.

FIG. 1.

FIG. 2.

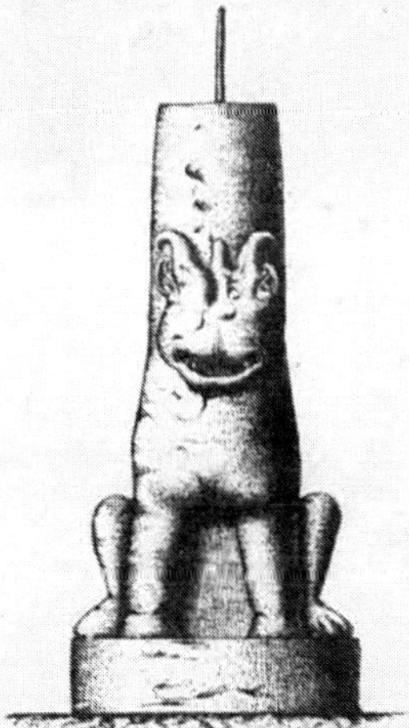

FIG. 3.

Scale of 12 9 6 3 0 1 2 3 4 5 Feet.

PLAN OF KAILÂSANÂHA TEMPLE. KÂÑCHÎPURAM. PLATE XXIV.

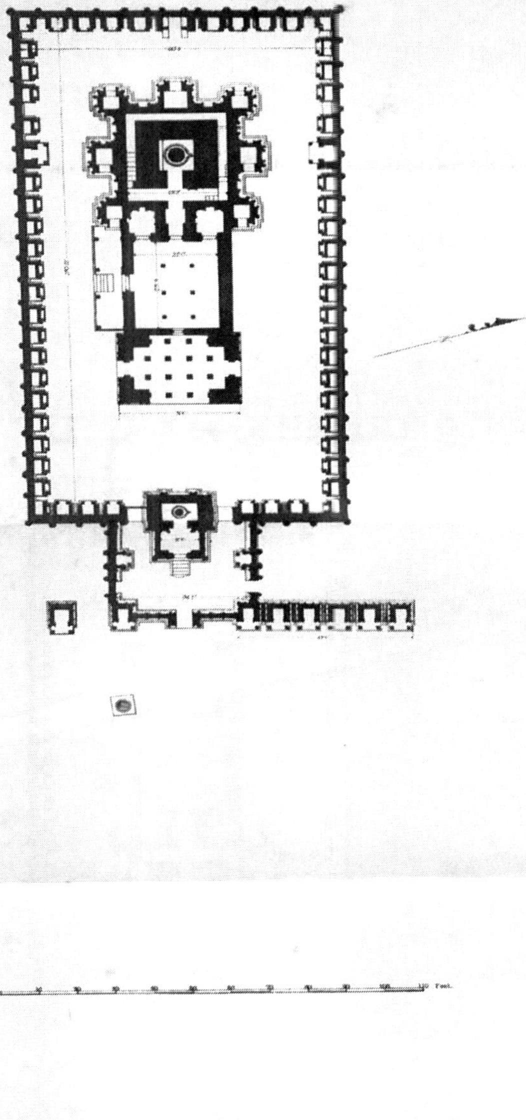

PLATE XXV.

KAILÂSÂNÂHA TEMPLE.
EAST EXTERIOR ELEVATION.
KÂÑCHÎPURAM.

PLATE XXVI.

KAILĀSANĀHA TEMPLE.
SOUTH ELEVATION.
KĀÑCHĪPURAM.

KAILÂSANÂHA TEMPLE.

EAST ELEVATION OF MAHÊNDRAVARMÂ SHRINE.

KÂÑCHÎPURAM.

PLATE XXVIII.

KAILÂSANÂDHA TEMPLE.

PANEL ON LEFT SIDE OF ENTRANCE TO GARBHAGRIHAM.

KÂÑCHÎPURAM.

Scale of 12 6 1 2 3 4 5 Feet

KAILÂSANÂDHA TEMPLE. PLATE XXIX.

PANEL ON LEFT EAST DOORWAY TO LARGE COURTYARD.

KÂÑCHÎPURAM.

Scale of 12 6 1 2 3 Feet.

KAILÂSANÂDHA TEMPLE. PLATE XXX.

PANEL ON RIGHT EAST DOORWAY TO LARGE COURT.

KÂÑCHÎPURAM.

Scale of 12 6 1 2 3 Feet.

PLATE XXXI.

KAILÂSANÂHA TEMPLE

East Interior Elevation of Courtyard.

KÂÑCHÎPURAM.

KAILÂSANÂDHA TEMPLE.

PANELS ON SOUTH SIDE OF COURT (NOS. 2 AND 3 FROM EAST END).

KÂÑCHÎPURAM.

FIG. 1.

FIG. 2.

Scale of 12 6 1 2 3 4 5 Feet.

6TH AND 7TH PANELS FROM EAST END OF COURT, SOUTH SIDE.

KÂÑCHÎPURAM.

FIG. 1.

FIG. 2.

10TH AND 11TH PANELS FROM EAST END OF COURT SOUTH SIDE.

FIG. 3.

FIG. 4.

4TH AND 5TH PANELS FROM EAST END OF COURT, SOUTH

FIG. 5.

FIG. 6.

Scale of 12 9 6 3 1 2 3 4 5 6 7 8 Feet.

PLATE XXXIV

KAILÂSANÂDHA TEMPLE.

PANELS 12 AND 13 FROM EAST END OF SOUTH SIDE OF COURT.

KAÑCHÎPURAM.

PLATE XXXV.

KAILÂSANÂHA TEMPLE.

PANELS 14TH AND 15TH FROM EAST END OF SOUTH SIDE OF COURT.

KÂÑCHÎPURAM.

FIG. 1.

FIG. 2.

Scale of 12 6 0 1 2 3 4 5 6 7 Feet.

PLATE XXXVI.

KAILÂSANÂHA TEMPLE.

PANELS 16TH AND 17TH FROM EAST END OF SOUTH SIDE OF COURT.

KÂÑCHÎPURAM.

FIG. 1.

FIG. 2.

Scale of 12″ 6″ 1′ 2′ 3′ 4′ 5′ 6′ 7 Feet.

PLATE XXXVII.

KAILÂSANÂDHA TEMPLE.
SOUTH INTERIOR ELEVATION OF COURTYARD.
KAÑCHÎPURAM.

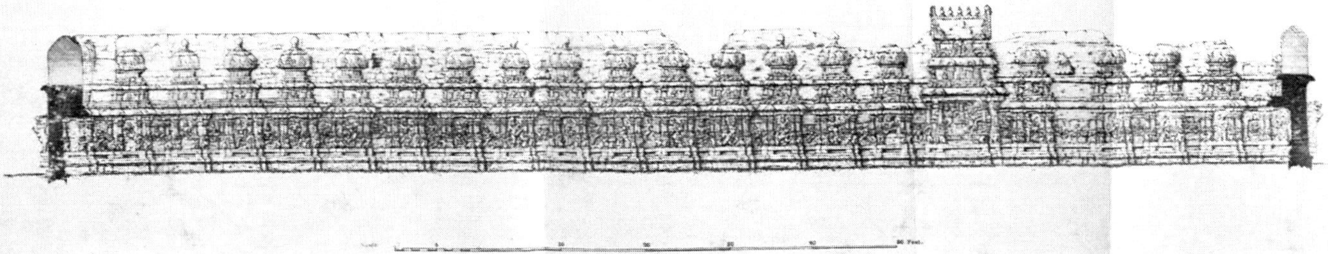

PLATE XXXVIII.

KAILÂSANÂDHA TEMPLE.

PANELS ON SOUTH SIDE OF COURT (NOS. 18 AND 19 FROM EAST END).

KÂÑCHÎPURAM.

FIG. 1.

FIG. 2.

Scale of 12 6 0 1 2 3 4 5 Feet.

PLATE XXXIX.

KAILÂSANÂHA TEMPLE.

KÂÑCHÎPURAM.

20TH PANEL FROM EAST END OF NORTH SIDE OF COURT.

FIG. 1.

PILLAR IN ARDDHAMANDAPAM.

FIG. 2.

Scale of 12 9 6 3 1 2 3 4 5 6 Feet.

Scale for Pillar.

10TH PANEL FROM EAST END OF WEST SIDE OF COURT.

FIG. 3.

21ST PANEL FROM EAST END OF NORTH SIDE OF COURT.

FIG. 4.

11TH PANEL FROM EAST END OF WEST SIDE OF COURT.

FIG. 5.

Scale of 12 9 6 3 1 2 3 4 5 6 7 8 9 Feet.

Scale for Panels

KAILÂSANÂDHA TEMPLE. PLATE XL.

PANELS 18 AND 19 FROM EAST END OF WEST SIDE OF COURT.

KAÑCHÎPURAM.

FIG. 1.

FIG. 2.

Scale of 12 9 6 3 1 2 3 4 5 6 7 Feet.

KAILÂSANÂDHA TEMPLE. PLATE XLI.

PANELS 16 AND 17 FROM END OF COURT, NORTH SIDE.

KAÑCHÎPURAM.

FIG. 1.

FIG. 2.

Scale of 12 6 0 1 2 3 4 5 6 Feet.

PLATE XLII.

KAILÂSANÂDHA TEMPLE.

PANELS ON NORTH SIDE OF COURT (NOS. 12 AND 13 FROM EAST END).

KÂÑCHÎPURAM.

FIG. 1.

FIG. 2.

KAILĀSANĀDHA TEMPLE.

PANELS ON NORTH SIDE OF COURT (NOS. 8 AND 9 FROM EAST END).

KĀÑCHĪPURAM.

FIG. 1.

FIG. 2.

Scale of 12 6 0 1 2 3 4 5 6 Feet.

PLATE XLIV.

KAILÂSANÂDHA TEMPLE.

PANELS ON NORTH SIDE OF COURT (NOS. 6 AND 7 FROM EAST END).

KÂÑCHÎPURAM.

FIG. 1.

FIG. 2.

Scale of 12 6 1 2 3 4 5 Feet.

KĀILASĀNADHA TEMPLE.

PLATE XLV.

PANELS ON NORTH SIDE OF COURT (NOS. 4 AND 5 FROM EAST END).

KĀÑCHĪPURAM.

FIG. 1.

FIG. 2.

Scale of 12 6 0 1 2 3 4 5 Feet.

KAILÂSANÂDHA TEMPLE. PLATE XLVI.

PANELS ON FRONT OF 2ND & 3RD CELLS FROM EAST END OF LARGE COURT (NORTH SIDE).

KÂÑCHÎPURAM.

FIG. 1.

FIG. 2.

Scale of 12 6 1 2 3 4 5 Feet.

KAILĀSANĀTHA TEMPLE.

NORTH INTERIOR ELEVATION OF COURTYARD.

KAÑCHĪPURAM.

PLATE XLVII

PLATE XLVIII.

KAILÁSANÁHA TEMPLE.

PIER IN MAHAMANDAPAM.

KAÑCHÍPURAM.

FIG. 1.

A CELL ON SOUTH SIDE OF COURT.

FIG. 2.

KAILÂSANÂDHA TEMPLE. PLATE XLIX.

WINDOW IN EAST END OF ARDDHAMAṆḌAPAM.

KÂÑCHÎPURAM.

Scale of 12 6 0 1 2 3 4 Feet.

KAILASANAHA TEMPLE.

EAST ELEVATION OF MAHAMANDAPAM.

KÃÑCHÎPURAM.

KAILÂSANÂHA TEMPLE.

PANEL 1ST TO RIGHT OF BACK CENTRAL SHRINE.

KÂNCHÎPURAM.

FIG. 1.

Scale of 12 9 6 3 0 1 2 3 4 5 Feet.

PANEL ON NORTH SIDE OF MAHAMANDAPAM.

FIG. 2

Scale of 9 6 3 0 1 2 3 4 5 6 7 Feet.

PLATE LII.

TRIPURANTAKÊSVARA TEMPLE.
PANEL ON BACK OF THE SHRINE.
KÂÑCHÎPURAM.

SECTION.

FIG. 1.

KAILÂSANÂHA TEMPLE
PANCHALÔGA IMAGES.
FIG. 2.

VALLI. SUBRAMANYA. DEVANAI.

Scale of [illegible] 3 6 9 12 15 Feet

SOMASKANDDAH.
FIG. 3.

PANDAVA PERUMAL TEMPLE.
YALI BASE.

SIDE. FIG. 4 FRONT.

FIG. 5.

PIER LYING ON GROUND NEAR VAIKUNTHAPERUMAL TEMPLE.

FIG. 6.

PIER STANDING IN MAIN STREET OF VISHNU KANCHI.

Scale of 12 9 6 3 1 2 3 4 5 6 7 8 Feet
Scale for Panel 2 Yalis, and Somaskandah.

Scale of 5 4 3 2 1 5 10 Feet
Scale for Piers.

KAILÂSANÂDHA TEMPLE. PLATE LIII.

PANEL IN SHRINE AT NORTH-WEST CORNER OF VIMÂNA.

KAÑCHÎPÛRAM.

Scale of 12 6 0 1 2 3 4 5 Feet.

KAILÂSÂNADHA TEMPLE.

PANEL ON NORTH SIDE OF SHRINE AT NORTH-WEST CORNER OF VIMÂNA,

KÂÑCHÎPURAM.

Scale of 12 6 1 2 3 4 5 6 7 Feet.

PLATE LV.

KAILASANAHA TEMPLE.

KÂÑCHÎPURAM.

PANEL 2ND FROM NORTH-WEST CORNER OF VIMANA, NORTH SIDE.

FIG. 1.

PANEL 3RD FROM NORTH-WEST CORNER OF VIMANA, NORTH SIDE.

FIG. 2.

Scale of 12 6 0 1 2 3 4 5 6 7 Feet

Scale for 2 Panels.

KAILÂSANÂDHATEMPLE. PLATE LVI.

4TH PANEL FROM NORTH-WEST CORNER OF VIMÂNA, NORTH SIDE.

KÂÑCHÎPURAM.

Scale of 12 6 1 2 3 4 5 Feet.

KAILÂSANÂDHA TEMPLE. PLATE LVII.

PANEL ON NORTH SIDE OF VIMANA, 5TH FROM NORTH-WEST CORNER.

KÂÑCHÎPURAM.

Scale of 12 6 0 1 2 3 4 5 6 7 Feet.

KAILÂSANÂDHA TEMPLE.

PLATE LVIII.

2ND PANEL FROM NORTH-WEST CORNER OF VIMÂNA, WEST SIDE.

KAṄCHÎPURAM.

Scale of 12 9 6 3 1 2 3 4 5 6 Feet.

KAILÂSANÂDHA TEMPLE. PLATE LIX.

Panel in Central Shrine on West Side of Vimāna.

KAÑCHIPŪRAM.

Scale of 12 6 1 2 3 4 5 Feet.

KAILÂSANÂDHA TEMPLE. PLATE LX.

2ND PANEL FROM SOUTH-WEST CORNER OF VIMÂNA, SOUTH SIDE.

KAÑCHÎPURAM.

Scale of 12 9 6 3 1 2 3 4 5 6 7 8 9 Feet.

KAILÂSANÂDHA TEMPLE. PLATE LXI.

PANEL ON BACK OF SHRINE AT SOUTH-WEST CORNER OF VIMÂNA.

KÂÑCHÎPURAM.

Scale of 12 6 1 2 3 4 5 Feet

KAILÂSANÂDHATEMPLE. PLATE LXII.

PANEL ON FRONT OF CENTER SHRINE, SOUTH SIDE OF VIMÂNA.

KÂÑCHÎPURAM.

Scale of 12 6 1 2 3 4 5 Feet.

PLATE LXIII.

VAIKUṆṬHAPERUMÂL TEMPLE.
Cross Section through Vimana.
KÂÑCHÎPURAM.

GROUND PLAN OF VAIKUNTHAPERUMAL TEMPLE. PLATE LXIV.

KÂÑCHÎPURAM.

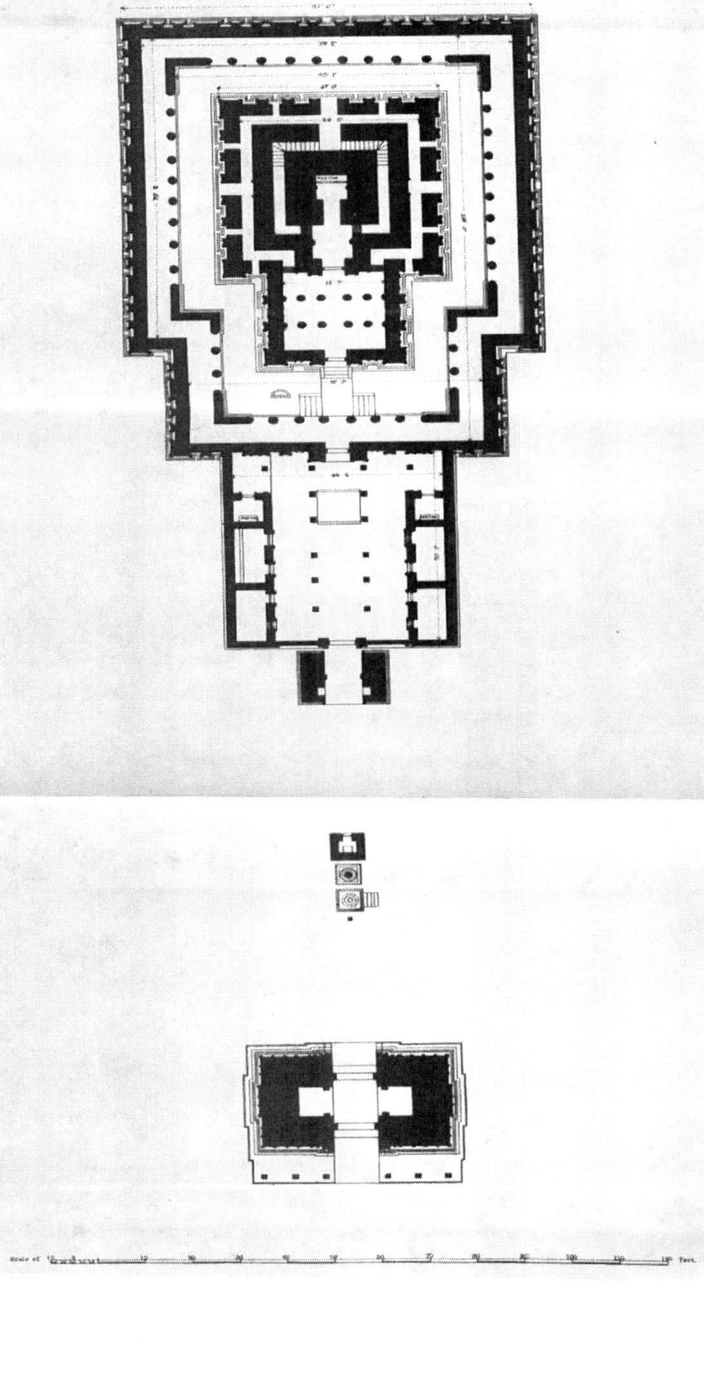

PLATE LXVI.

VAIKUNṬHAPERUMAL TEMPLE.

ELEVATION OF EXTERIOR COURTWALL NEAR NORTH-WEST CORNER.

KÂÑCHÎPURAM.

Scale of 10 5 10 20 Feet.

PLATE LXVII.

VAIKUNṬHA PERUMÂL TEMPLE.

SCULPTURE ON TOP OF A NICHE ON SOUTH EXTERIOR SIDE OF COURT WALL.

KÂÑCHÎPURAM.

Scale of 12 6 1 2 Feet

PLATE LXVIII.

VAIKUṆṬHA PERUMÂL TEMPLE.

PILLAR AND PANEL IN WEST PORCH.

KÂÑCHÎPURAM.

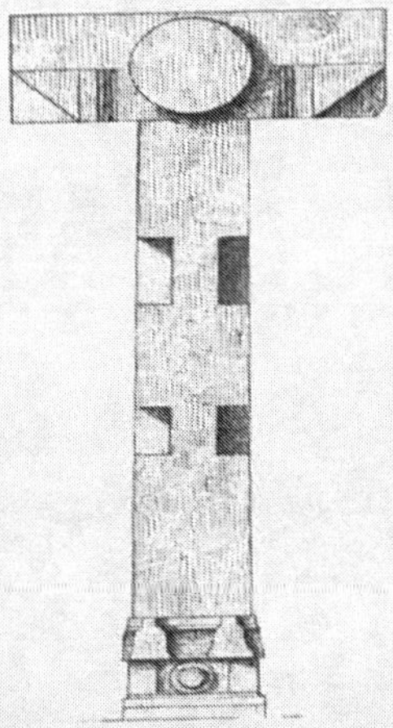

FIG. 1.

Scale of 12 9 6 3 . 1 2 3 4 5 6 Feet.

FIG. 2.

Scale of 12 11 10 9 8 7 6 5 4 3 2 1 . 1 Foot.

VAIKUṆṬHAPERUMÂL TEMPLE.

PANEL ON EAST SIDE OF INNER SHRINE WALL.

KÂÑCHÎPURAM.

PANEL ON NORTH SIDE OF 2ND INNER SHRINE WALL.

FIG. 1.

Scale of 12 1 2 3 4 5 6 7 8 9 Feet

FIG. 2.

VAIKUṆṬHAPERUMÂL TEMPLE.

5TH PANEL TO LEFT OF CENTRE OF 3RD NORTH SHRINE WALL

FIG. 3.

MUKTÊŚVARA TEMPLE.

NANDI MANDAPA.

FIG. 4.

VAIKUṆṬHAPERUMÂL TEMPLE.

PANEL AT ENTRANCE DOOR.

FIG. 5.

Scale of 12 6 1 2 Feet Scale of 12 0 1 2 3 4 5 6 7 8 9

Scale of 12 6 1 Feet

VAIKUNṬHAPERUMÂḶ TEMPLE. PLATE LXX.

Panel on South Side of 2nd Inner Shrine Wall.

KÂÑCHÎPURAM.

Scale of 12 6 1 2 3 4 5 6 7 8 9 Feet.

VAIKUNTHAPERUMAL TEMPLE.

PLATE LXXI.

PANEL AT SOUTH-WEST CORNER OF WEST WALL OF SHRINE.

KÂÑCHÎPURAM.

TWO PANELS ON SOUTH WALL OF ARDHAMANDAPAM.

FIG. 1.

FIG. 2.

FIG.

5TH PANEL TO LEFT OF CENTRE 3RD NORTH SHRINE WALL.

FIG. 4.

6TH PANEL TO RIGHT OF CENTRE OF 3RD EAST SHRINE WALL.

FIG. 5.

1ST PANEL TO LEFT OF CENTRE OF 3RD SHRINE WALL, SOUTH SIDE.

FIG. 6.

Scale of 12 6 1 2 3 4 5 6 7 8 9 10 Feet.

PLATE LXXII.

VAIKUNṬHAPERUMÂḶ TEMPLE.

5TH PANEL TO LEFT OF CENTRE OF 3RD (OUTER) SHRINE WALL, SOUTH SIDE.

KÂÑCHÎPURAM.

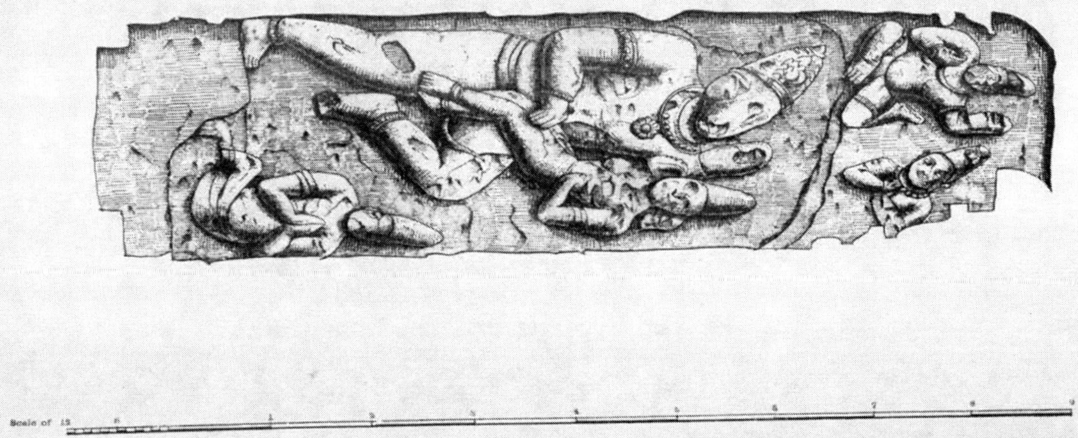

VAIKUNṬHAPERUMÂḶ TEMPLE. PLATE LXXIII.

2ND PANEL TO RIGHT OF CENTER OF 3RD NORTH SHRINE WALL.

KÂÑCHÎPURAM.

Scale of 12 6 0 1 2 3 4 5 6 7 Feet.

PLATE LXXIV.

VAIKUNTHAPERUMÂL TEMPLE.

Panels on 1st Storey of Vimâna Nos. 16, 17, and 18, to Right of South-West Corner

KÂÑCHÎPURAM.

Fig. 1.

Fig. 2

Fig. 3

VAIKUNTHAPERUMÂL TEMPLE

2nd Panel at Left of Centre of 3rd North Shrine

MATANGÊŚVARA TEMPLE

Left Panel in Porch.

Fig. 4.

Fig. 5.

Scale of 12 6 0 1 2 3 4 5 6 7 8 9 10 11 Feet

Scale for all the Panels.

VAIKUNTHAPERUMÂL TEMPLE. PLATE LXXV.

6TH PANEL TO RIGHT OF CENTRE E, 2ND SHRINE WALL.

KÂÑCHÎPURAM.

Scale of 12 9 6 3 1 2 3 4 5 6 7 8 Feet.

VAIKUṆṬHA PERUMÂḶ TEMPLE.

1ST AND 3RD PANELS TO LEFT OF CENTRE ON NORTH 3RD SHRINE WALL.

5TH PANEL TO RIGHT OF CENTRE ON NORTH 3RD SHRINE WALL.

KÂÑCHÎPURAM.

FIG. 1.

FIG. 2.

FIG. 3.

Scale of 12 6 1 2 3 4 5 6 7 8 9 10 Feet.

VAIKUṆṬHAPERUMÂL TEMPLE.

PLATE LXXVII.

PANEL ON SHRINE WALLS.

KÂÑCHÎPURAM.

THIRD SOUTH WALL OF SHRINE.

2ND TO RIGHT OF CENTRE.

FIG. 1.

5TH TO RIGHT OF CENTRE.

FIG. 2.

6TH TO RIGHT OF CENTRE.

FIG. 3.

THIRD EAST WALL OF SHRINE.

2ND TO LEFT OF CENTRE.

FIG. 4.

2ND TO RIGHT OF CENTRE

FIG. 5.

5TH TO RIGHT OF CENTRE.

FIG. 6.

Scale of 12 6 0 1 2 3 4 5 6 7 8 9 10 Feet

VAIKUṆṬHA PERUMÂL TEMPLE. PLATE LXXVIII.

5TH AND 6TH PANELS TO LEFT OF CENTRE ON EAST FACE OF 3RD SHRINE WALL. 6TH PANEL TO RIGHT OF CENTRE ON SOUTH FACE OF 3RD SHRINE WALL.

KÂÑCHÎPURAM.

FIG. 1.

FIG. 2.

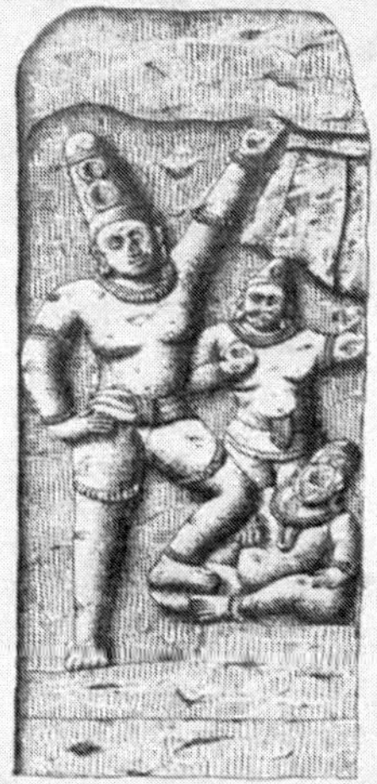

FIG. 3.

Scale of 12 6 0 1 2 3 4 5 6 7 8 9 Feet

VAIKUNṬHA PERUMÂL TEMPLE.

Corner Panels on South Wall of Arddhamaṇḍapam. 1st and 2nd Panels from South-West Corner on West Wall of Arddhamaṇḍapam.

KÂÑCHÎPURAM.

Fig. 1.

Fig. 2.

Fig. 3.

Scale of 12 — 1 2 3 4 5 6 7 8 9 10 Feet.

VAIKUṆṬHAPERUMÂL TEMPLE. PLATE LXXX.

NORTH-WEST CORNER OF ARDDHAMAṆḌAPAM, 2ND CORNER PANELS ON PROJECTION

KÂÑCHÎPURAM.

FIG. 1.

FIG. 2.

1ST PANEL TO RIGHT ON WEST WALL OF ARDDHAMAṆḌAPAM.

FIG. 3.

PANELS TO RIGHT OF SOUTH-WEST CORNER OF 1ST STOREY OF VIMÂNA.

8TH PANEL.

FIG. 4.

9TH PANEL.

FIG. 5.

10TH PANEL.

FIG. 6.

11TH PANEL.

FIG. 7.

Scale of 12 6 0 1 2 3 4 5 6 7 8 9 10 12 Feet

VAIKUNṬHA PERUMÂḶ TEMPLE. PLATE LXXXI.

FOUR PANELS ON SOUTH SIDE OF 1ST STOREY OF VIMÂNA—TO RIGHT OF SOUTH-WEST CORNER.

KÂÑCHÎPURAM.

FIG. 1.

FIG. 2.

FIG. 3.

FIG. 4.

Scale of 12 1 2 3 4 5 6 7 8 9 10 Feet.

VAIKUṆṬHA PERUMÂL TEMPLE. PLATE LXXXII.

PANELS ON 1ST STOREY OF VIMÂNA 5TH TO 7TH TO RIGHT OF SOUTH-WEST CORNER.

KÂÑCHÎPURAM.

FIG. 1.

FIG. 2.

FIG. 3.

Scale of 12 9 6 3 1 2 3 4 5 6 7 8 9 10 11 12 Feet.

PLATE LXXXIII.

VAIKUṆṬHA PERUMÂL TEMPLE.

PANELS ON 1ST STOREY OF VIMÂNA 12TH TO 15TH TO RIGHT OF SOUTH-WEST CORNER.

KÂÑCHÎPURAM.

FIG. 1.

FIG. 2.

FIG. 3.

FIG. 4.

Scale of 12 6 . 1 2 3 4 5 6 7 8 9 10 Feet.

PANELS ON 1ST STOREY OF VIMÂNA 19TH TO 22ND TO RIGHT OF SOUTH-WEST CORNER.

KÃÑCHÎPURAM.

FIG. 1.

FIG. 2.

FIG. 3.

FIG. 4

PANEL ON WEST SHRINE WALL AT NORTH-WEST CORNER.

FIG. 5.

2 RECESSED PANELS ON NORTH WALL OF ARDDHAMANDAPAM.

FIG. 6

FIG. 7.

Scale of 12 9 6 3 . 1 2 3 4 5 6 7 8 9 10 Feet

PLATE LXXXV.

VAIKUṆṬHAPERUMĀL TEMPLE.
SIDE ELEVATION OF
KĀÑCHĪPURAM.

PLATE LXXXVI.

VAIKUṆṬHA PERUMÂL TEMPLE.

FIGURES IN THE 1ST STOREY OF VIMÂNA.

KÂÑCHÎPURAM.

FIG. 1.

FIG. 2.

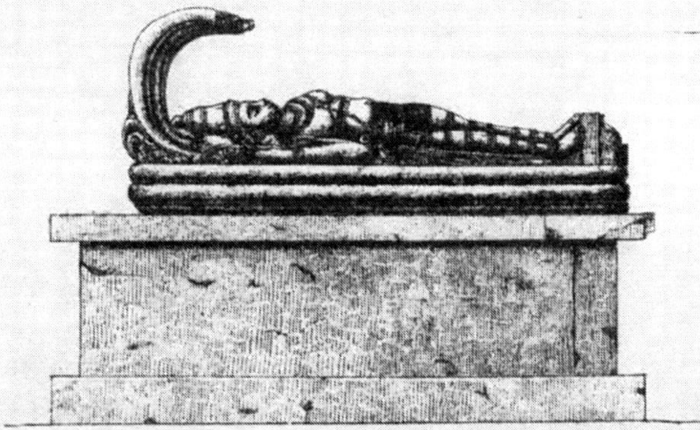

FIG. 3.

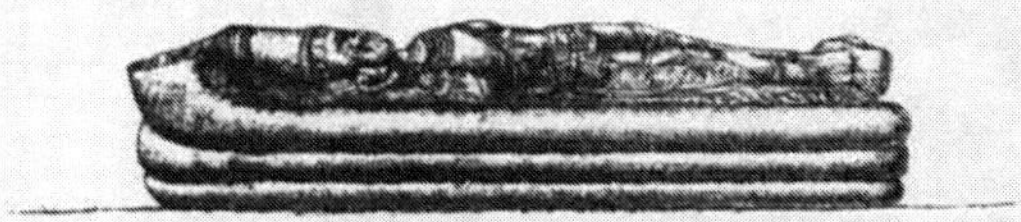

FIG. 4.

Scale of 12 6 . 1 2 3 4 5 6 Feet

PLATE LXXXVII

VAIKUNTHAPERUMAL TEMPLE.

1 PIER IN WEST VERANDA IN COURTYARD. (FRONT AND SIDE).

KANCHIPURAM.

2 PIERS IN ANTARALAMANDAPAM. (FRONT AND SIDE).

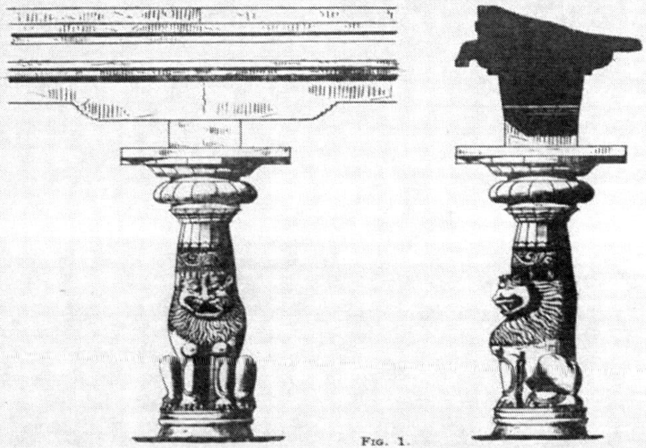

FIG. 1.

FIG. 2.

Scale of 12 6 . 1 2 3 4 5 6 7 8 9 10 11 Feet

VAIKUNTHAPERUMĀL TEMPLE. PLATE LXXXVIII.

2 Panels on Inside of West-North Wall at North-West Corner.

KAÑCHIPURAM.

PLATE LXXXIX.

VAIKUNṬHAPERUMÂL TEMPLE.

PANELS ON TWO WALLS AT SOUTH-WEST CORNER OF COURT.

KÂNCHÎPURAM.

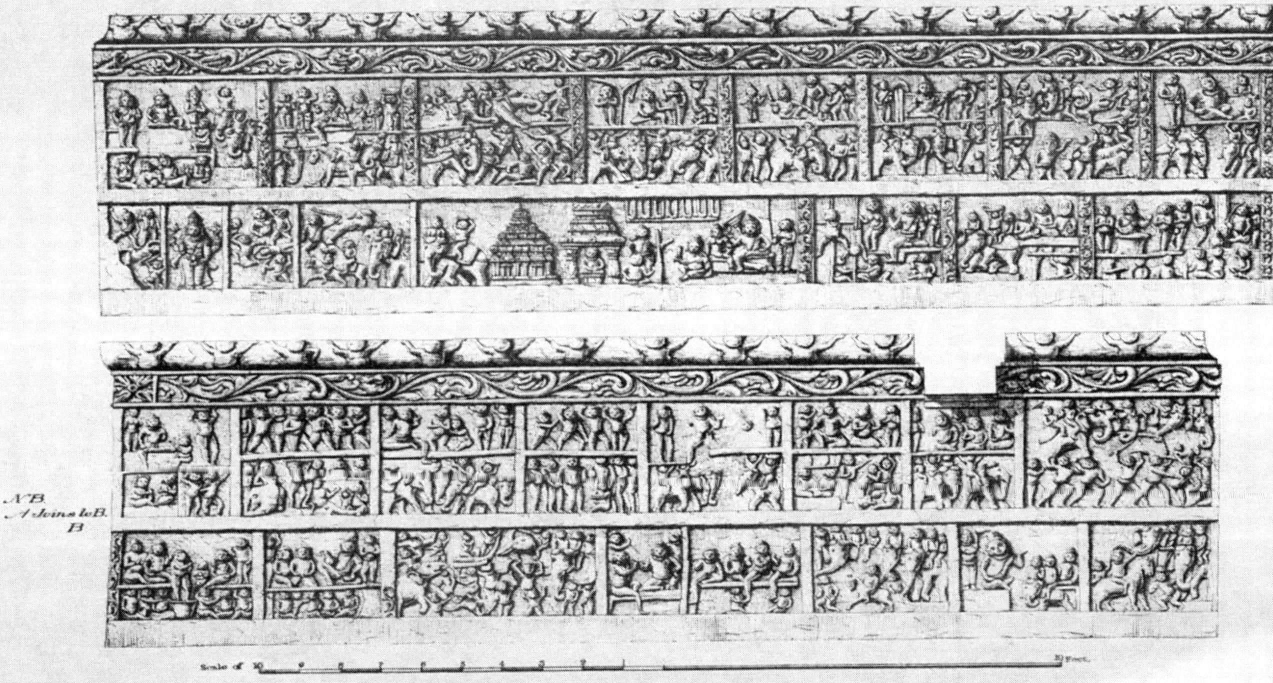

PLATE XC.

VAIKUNTHAPERUMAL TEMPLE.
PANELS ON SOUTH WALL OF COURT.
KĀÑCHĪPURAM

FIG. 2.

NB.—A. Joins to B. and C. Joins to D.

On return wall at South-West Corner.

FIG. 1.

FIG. 3.

Scale of ... 30 Feet.

PLATE XCI.

VAIKUNTHAPERUMÂL TEMPLE.

PANELS OF NORTH WALL AND SMALL RETURN WALL AT WEST OF COURT.

KÂÑCHÎPURAM.

D

Fig.

N.B.—A Joins to B and C Joins to D.

A

Fig. 2.

B

C

Fig. 3.

Scale of ... Feet

PLATE XCIII.

VAIKUNTHAPERUMÂL TEMPLE.
PANEL ON EAST WALL OF COURT,
KÂÑCHÎPURAM.

FIG. 1.

A Joins to B.

FIG. 2.

Scale of 10 9 8 7 6 5 4 3 2 1 10 20 feet.

PLAN OF MATANGÊŚVARA TEMPLE. PLATE XCIII.

KÂÑCHÎPURAM.

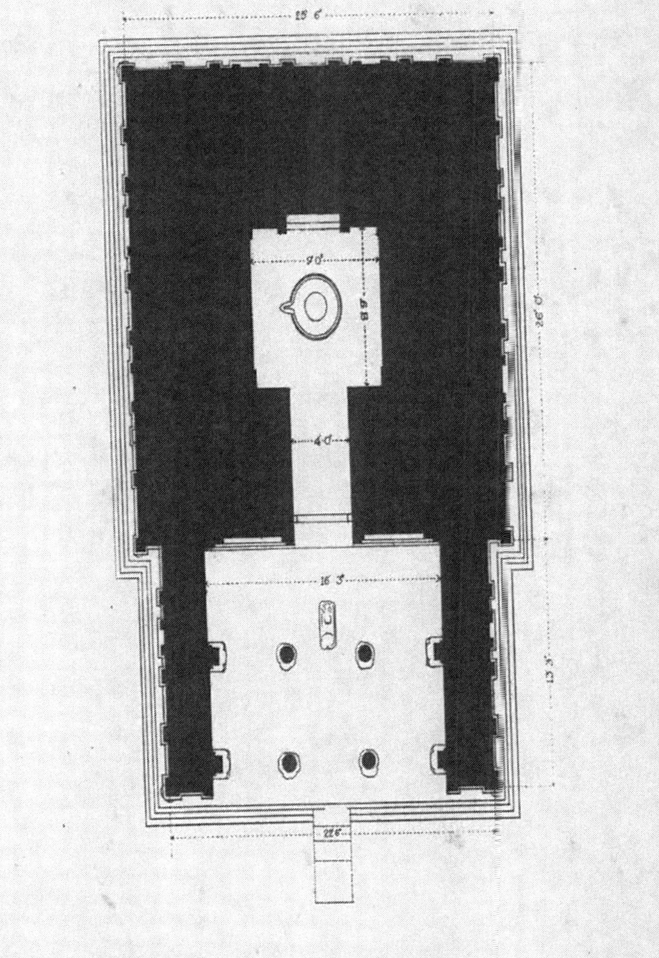

PLATE XCIV.

MATANGÊŚVARA TEMPLE.

PANELS ON SIDE WALLS OF GARBHAGRIHAM.

KÂÑCHÎPURAM.

PLATE XCV.

MATANGÊŚVARA TEMPLE.

PANELS IN ANTARÂLA MAṆḌAPAM.

KÂÑCHÎPURAM.

Scale of 12 | 1 2 3 4 5 6 7 8 9 10 11 12 13 14 15 16 17 Feet.

MATANGÊŚVARA TEMPLE. PLATE XCVI.

PANELS ON BACK OF GARBHAGRIHAM.

KÂÑCHÎPURAM.

Scale of 12 6 · 1 2 3 4 5 6 7 Feet.

MUKTESVARA TEMPLE. PLATE XCVII.

PANELS AT RIGHT OF PORCH.

KÂÑCHÎPURAM

FIG. 1.

MATANGÊSVARA TEMPLE.

PANELS AT RIGHT OF PORCH.

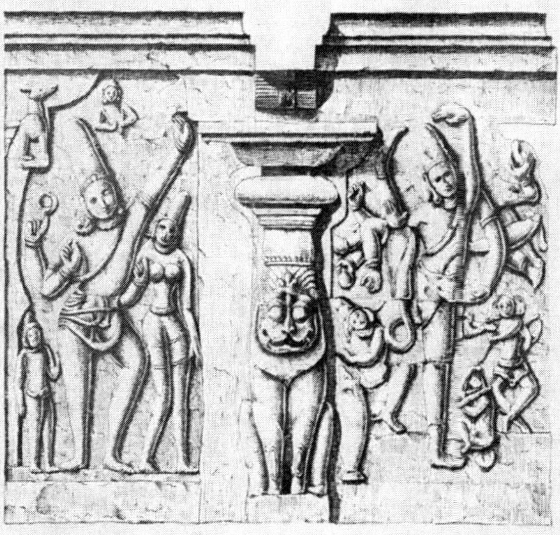

FIG. 2.

Scale of 12 6 0 1 2 3 4 5 6 7 8 9 10 Feet

MATANGÊŚVARA TEMPLE. PLATE XCVIII.

INNER PILLAR IN THE ANTARÂLAMANDAPAM.

KÃÑCHÎPURAM.

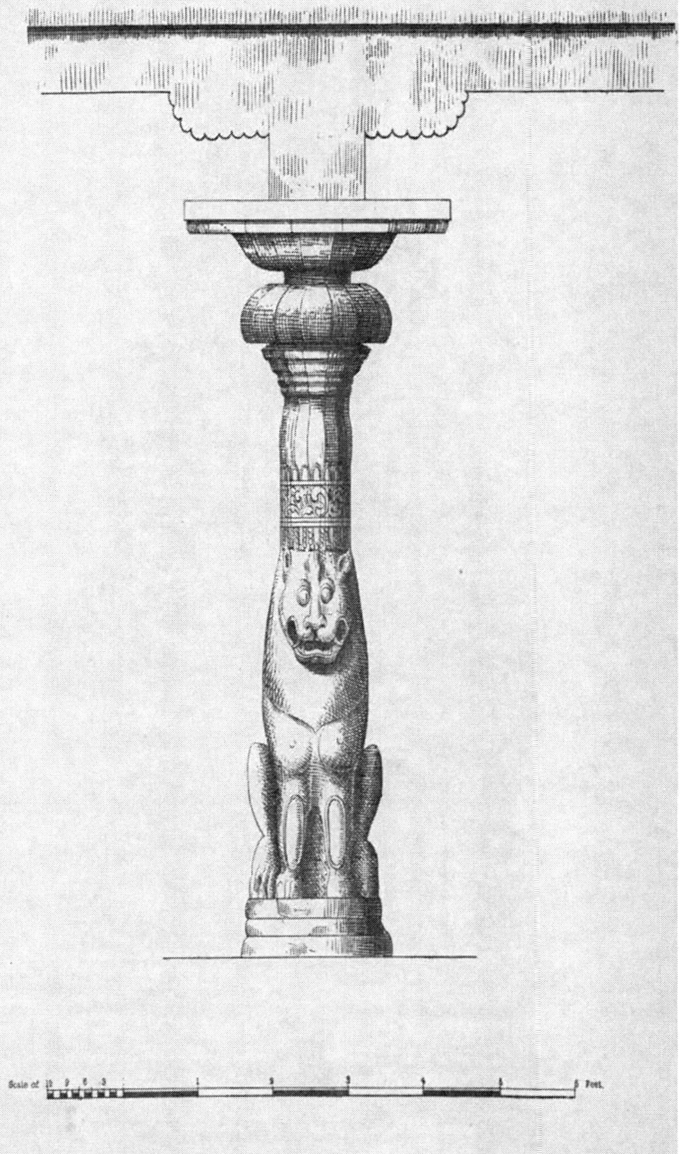

MATANGÊŚVARA TEMPLE.

PLATE XCIX.

West Elevation.

KÂÑCHÎPURAM

PLATE C.

MATAÑGEŚVARA TEMPLE.
North Elevation.
KAÑCHIPURAM.

PLAN OF MUKTÊŚVARA TEMPLE, KÂÑCHÎPURAM

PLATE CI.

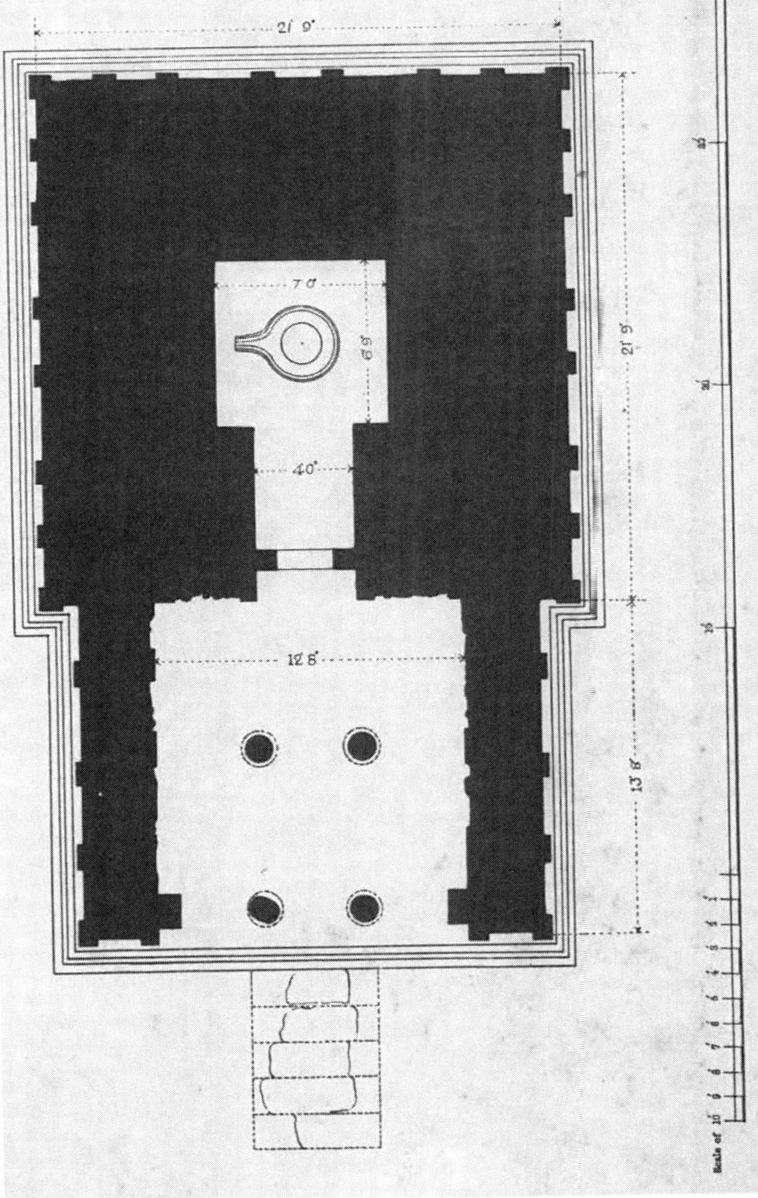

PLATE CII.

MUKTESVARA TEMPLE.
FRONT PILLAR IN THE PORCH.
KĀÑCHĪPURAM.

PLATE CIII.

MUKTÊŚVARA TEMPLE.

PANEL ON LEFT SIDE OF GARBHAGRIHAM.

KÂÑCHÎPURAM.

Scale of 12" 6" 0 1 2 3 4 5 6 Feet.

MUKTÊŚVARA TEMPLE. PLATE C V.

PANEL ON THE BACK OF THE SHRINE.

KÂÑCHÎPURAM.

FIG. 1.

Scale of 12 6 0 1 2 3 4 5 6 Feet

PANEL ON THE BACK OF THE PORCH.

FIG. 2.

Scale of 12 6 0 1 2 3 4 5 6 7 8 9 10 Feet.

MUKTÊŚVARA TEMPLE.

PANEL ON LEFT OF PORCH.

KÂÑCHÎPURAM.

PLATE CV.

MUKTÊSVARA TEMPLE.
FRONT ELEVATION
KÂÑCHÎPURAM.

MUKTÊŚVARA TEMPLE.

NORTH SIDE ELEVATION.

KÂÑCHÎPURAM.

PLATE CVII.

Scale of 10 9 8 7 6 5 4 3 2 1 0 10 20 Feet

TRIPURÂNTAKÊŚVARA TEMPLE. PLATE CVIII.
KÂÑCHÎPURAM.

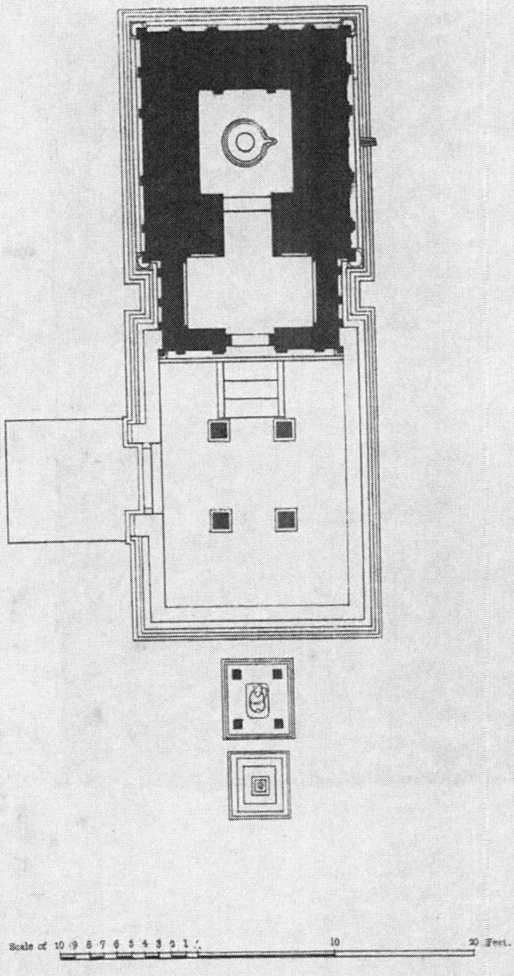

PLATE CIX.

TRIPURANTAKĒŚVARA TEMPLE.

PANELS IN ARDHAMAṆḌAPAM.

KÂÑCHÎPURAM.

FIG. 1.

FIG. 2.

Scale of 12 9 6 3 · 1 2 3 4 5 6 7 8 9 10 Feet.

PLATE CX.

TRIPURÂNTÂKÊŚVARA TEMPLE.

PANELS ON BACK OF ANTARALA MAṆḌAPAM.

KÂÑCHÎPURAM.

TRIPURÂNTAKÊŚVARA TEMPLE. PLATE CXI.*

Panels on West Side.

KÂÑCHÎPURAM.

Fig. 1.

Panels on North Side.

Fig. 2.

Scale of 12 6 0 1 2 3 4 5 6 7 8 9 10 Feet

TRIPURÂNTAKÊŚVARA TEMPLE.

PANELS ON SOUTH SIDE.

KÂÑCHÎPURAM.

PLATE CXII.

Scale of 12 6 0 1 2 3 4 5 6 7 8 9 10 11 12 13 Feet.

TRIPURÂNTAKÊŚVARA TEMPLE.

SIDE ELEVATION.

KÂÑCHÎPURAM.

PLATE CXIII

TRIPURĀNTAKĒŚVARA TEMPLE.

GANĒŚVARA AND THANDĒŚVARA.

KÂÑCHÎPURAM.

PLATE CXIV.

Fig. 1.

Fig. 2.

Scale of 12 9 6 3 1 2 Feet.

AIRÂVATÊŚVARA TEMPLE,
KÂÑCHÎPURAM.

PLATE CXV.

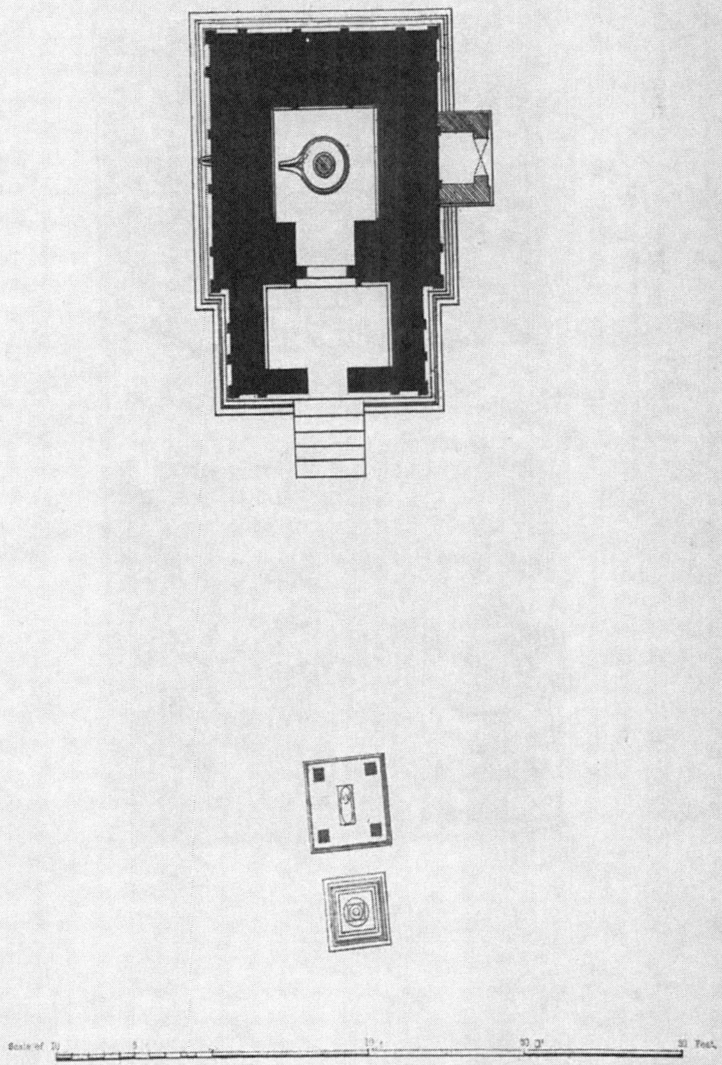

AIRĀVATÊŚVARA TEMPLE.
PANELS ON SIDES OF SHRINE.
KÂÑCHÎPŪRAM.

PLATE CXVI.

AIRÂVATÊŚVARA TEMPLE.

PLATE CXVII.

PANELS ON BACK OF GARBHAGRIHAM.

KÂÑCHÎPURAM.

Scale of 12 6 1 2 3 4 5 Feet.

AIRÂVATÊŚVARA TEMPLE.

PANELS ON BACK OF ANTARÂLAMANḌAPAM.

KÂÑCHÎPURAM.

FIG. 1.

Scale of 12 6 1 2 3 4 5 6 7 Feet.

AIRÂVATÊŚVARA TEMPLE.

PANELS ON SIDES OF ANTARÂLAMANḌAPAM.

KÂÑCHÎPURAM.

FIG. 2.

FIG. 3.

Scale of 12 6 1 2 3 4 5 6 7 Feet.

AIRÂVATÊŚVARA TEMPLE.

PANELS ON SIDE WALLS.

KÂÑCHÎPURAM.

PLATE CXIX.

ON NORTH SIDE.

FIG. 1.

ON SOUTH SIDE.

FIG. 2.

Scale of 12 9 6 3 1 2 3 4 5 6 7 8 Feet.

ADIKÊŚAVAPERUMÂL TEMPLE. PLATE CXX.

GROUND PLAN.

KÛRAM.

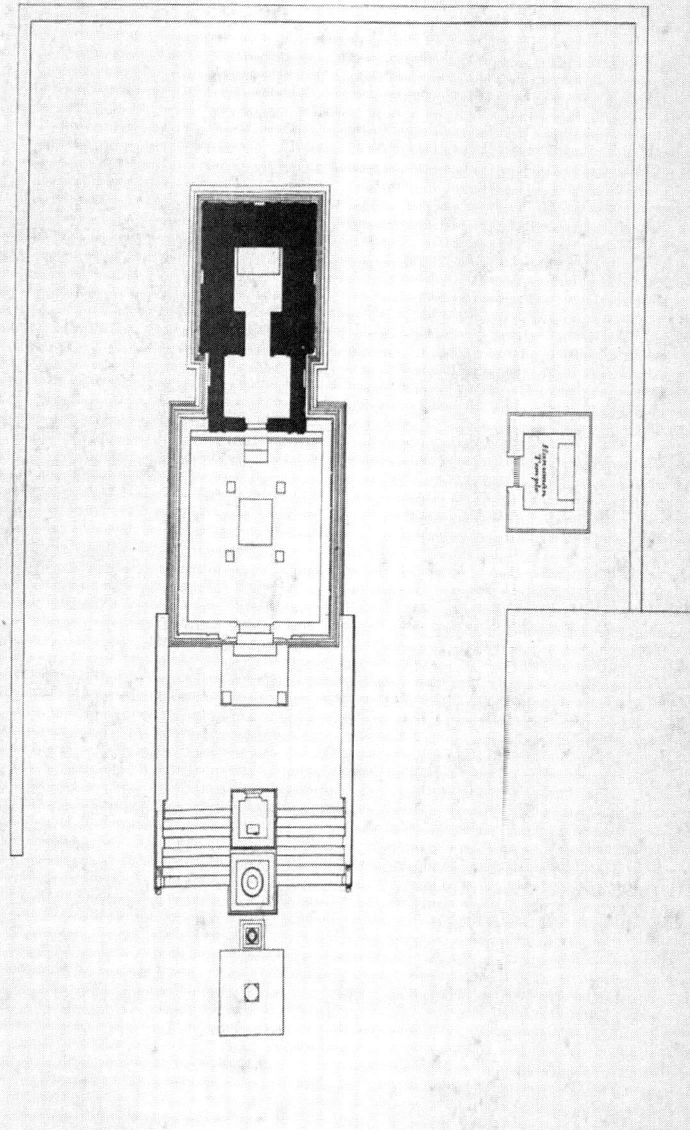

PLATE CXXI

AIKÊŚAVAPERUMÂL TEMPLE.
NORTH ELEVATION.
KÛRAM.

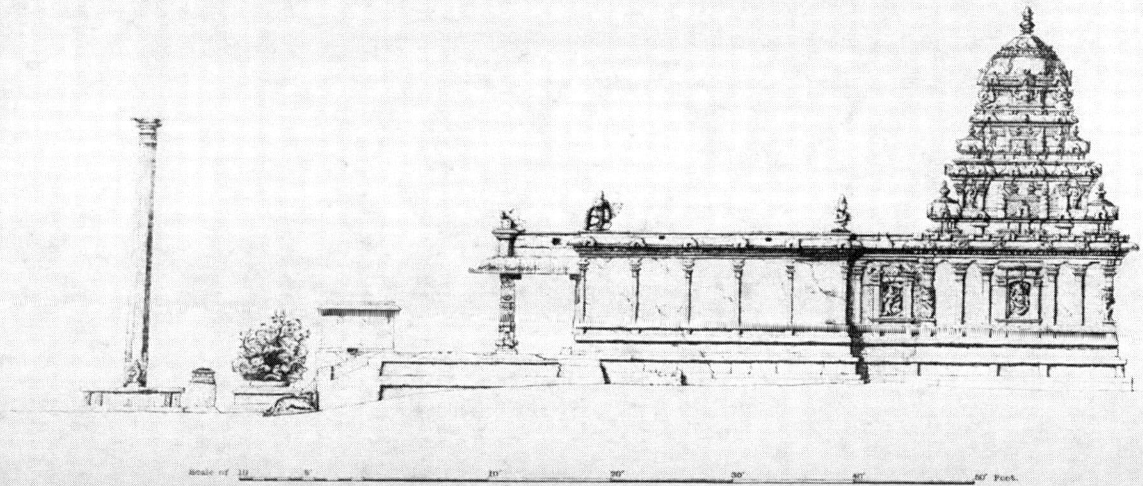

KACHÊŚVARA TEMPLE.

BLACK STONE WINDOW AT A SMALL SHRINE IN WEST END OF COURTYARD.

KÂÑCHÎPURAM.

Scale of 12 9 6 3 1 2 Feet.

KAILASANAHA TEMPLE. PLATE CXXIII.

PANELS 20TH, 21ST, AND 22ND FROM EAST END OF SOUTH SIDE OF COURT

KÂÑCHÎPURAM.

FIG. 1.

FIG 2

FIG. 3.

PANELS 14TH AND 15TH FROM EAST END OF NORTH SIDE OF COURT.

FIG. 4.

FIG. 5.

PANELS 8TH AND 9TH FROM EAST END OF SOUTH SIDE OF COURT.

FIG. 6.

FIG 7

Scale of 12 9 6 3 0 1 2 3 4 5 6 7 Feet

PLATE CXXIV.

KAILÂSANÂHA TEMPLE.

West Interior Elevation of Courtyard.

KÂÑCHÎPURAM.

Scale of 10' 5' 10' 20' 30' 40' Feet.